BUSINESS-GOVERNMENT RELATIONS AND INTERDEPENDENCE

Business-Government Relations and Interdependence

A MANAGERIAL AND ANALYTIC PERSPECTIVE

John M. Stevens,
Steven L. Wartick, and
John W. Bagby

QUORUM BOOKS

NEW YORK • WESTPORT, CONNECTICUT • LONDON

Library of Congress Cataloging-in-Publication Data

Stevens, John M.
   Business-government relations and interdependence : a managerial
and analytic perspective / John M. Stevens, Steven L. Wartick, and
John W. Bagby.
      p.   cm.
   Bibliography: p.
   Includes index.
   ISBN 0–89930–310–2 (lib. bdg. : alk. paper)
   1. Industry and state.   2. Industry and state—United States.
I. Wartick, Steven Leslie.   II. Bagby, John W.   III. Title.
HD3611.S765 1988
338.973—dc19   87–32279

British Library Cataloguing in Publication Data is available.

Library of Congress Catalog Card Number: 87-32279
ISBN: 0–89930–310–2

First published in 1988 by Quorum Books

Greenwood Press, Inc.
88 Post Road West, Westport, Connecticut 06881

Printed in the United States of America

The paper used in this book complies with the
Permanent Paper Standard issued by the National
Information Standards Organization (Z39.48–1984).

10   9   8   7   6   5   4   3   2   1

Contents

Figures and Tables

FIGURES

TABLES

Acknowledgments

The authors wish to acknowledge the many individuals and organizations who so graciously gave of their time and knowledge
in helping us to pursue and understand the elusive concept of
business-government relations. The primary contributors to our
study were, of course, the public and private managers who participated in the interview or survey portion of the project. This
participation evolved from their sincere desire to improve the
interactions between the dominant forces in our society, namely,
government and business. Their original commitment, experience, and desire to leave a practical and intellectual heritage
based upon their work with the Governor's Management Improvement Project (GMIP) in New Jersey is respected by the authors. We can only hope that we have done justice to their
objectives with the reporting in this book. In a sense, we cannot
hope to capture all of the subtleties inherent in such a complex
interplay of forces, but we owe it to the participants to try because
it was a program that taught lessons with great potential payoffs
for all of us.

Though we take the chance of missing important actors in the
process of which we were outside observers, the following individuals are those whom we wish to acknowledge. Our inability
to identify all of the key people in the process is admittedly our
shortcoming for which we apologize in advance. The following
order is mostly chronological and not designed to denote any
particular hierarchy. In the inception phase of this study, Carole
Kottmeier was sensitive enough to recognize the special character
of this unique undertaking and to focus upon the positive rather

than negative dimensions of human interaction. At the initiation of the process, Governor Thomas Kean, Alfred E. Fasola, Director of the Governor's Office of Management Services; Rocco Marano, then president of New Jersey Bell; David R. Clare, president of Johnson and Johnson; and Robert R. Ferguson, Jr., chief executive officer of First National Bank Bancorp, were core leaders in the design and implementation of the project.

Richard B. Standiford, Director and Comptroller, Division of Budget and Accounting, State of New Jersey, demonstrated exceptional leadership, cooperation, and commitment to deriving the most beneficial lessons from the study. Michael O'Neal, Director, Division of Planning, provided the early vision and support that permitted the benefits of a study such as this to occur. Alfred B. Gaissert, Project Director of the Paperwork Management Program, provided the insight that only an informed observer can provide. James Alexander, Jr., Director of Administration, Department of Community Affairs; Sidney Ytkin, Assistant Commissioner for Management and Budget, Department of Environmental Protection; and John Repko, Director of Marketing, Department of Agriculture, deserve special mention for explaining the complexity of the "real world" of management and identifying the need not to forget the potential of continuity in pursuing the positive aspects of business-government interdependence. They increased our faith in the ability of informed managers to do the right things and in subtle ways lead theory.

We wish to thank our colleagues in the Departments of Public Administration and Business Logistics at the Pennsylvania State University for their administrative and collegial support throughout the study. Ali Pamir, Leonard Omolecki, Judy Sartore, Barbara Lippincott, Janette Barger, Beth Ondo, Carol Coppolino, and others helped transform ideas, data, analyses, and sometimes fuzzy or illegible writing into more coherent, organized text and tables. The cooperation, guidance, help, and attention to detail provided by Eric Valentine and Penny Sippel of Greenwood Press were critical and are gratefully acknowledged. Our families deserve special recognition because of their commitment as the number of projects outside the families grow. We also want to give blanket recognition to those we may have not explicitly identified and who have helped us further refine the need to explore the growing, critical interdependence between important managerial elements in our society.

BUSINESS-GOVERNMENT
RELATIONS AND
INTERDEPENDENCE

CHAPTER 1

Business-Government Relations and Interdependence: In Search of an Exploratory Framework

Business has generally blamed its problems on so-called opportunistic politicians, rapacious bureaucrats, misinformed do-gooders, and a duped public. The fault is always with "them," not "us." But there is a chance that Cassius was right: "The fault, dear Brutus, is not in our stars, but in ourselves." Consider what would be the reaction of a corporation president with a division manager who habitually blamed his repeated losses on the actions of his competitors. The president would surely think such a chronic loser must have only himself to blame. "Early retirement" would be his early fate.

It is my thesis that the blame for the chronic defeats of business lie as much with business as with its "competitors," that perhaps business has made the mistake, not of fighting its competition poorly (it is too well practiced in the arts of competition), but of fighting competition when it should more frequently have joined it. And I have for all this a "marketing" explanation.

THEODORE LEVITT
in "Why Business Always Loses"
Harvard Business Review

PURPOSE AND APPROACH

There has been increasing cynicism regarding the morality, effectiveness, ideology, and role of corporations in the intellectual, business, and public communities. This attitude is not new in the United States, but the current manifestations of many long-standing issues are taking shape in the problematic relationships between business and government. Efforts at dealing with international competition, insider trading, deregulation, and re-regulation implicitly address the question of whether business is efficient in defining and achieving its objectives overall, including its relationship with governmental bodies. The traditional theory of the firm or corporation does not appear to address the growing complexity associated with a multiple constituent and stakeholder context that characterizes the environment of contemporary business and government. The primary incremental, battling business or arms-length approaches to business-government relations (BGR) have not been adequate in dealing with the perplexing intricacy inherent in either the pragmatic or the theoretical aspects of government-business interdependence. One purpose of this book is an attempt to further identify and reformulate the issues and problems, using a data-based analytical and managerial approach that converges on substantive issues.

If business can be held responsible for its own problems, as stated by Levitt, then the same judgment may apply to the managerial components of the governmental counterpart in the interaction. Currently, much of the written work describing BGR is either unidimensional in emphasizing one sector over the other, or ambiguous in treating the bases of interactions. Some literature is oriented toward specific facets of BGR, such as regulation (Mitnick, 1980) or legal issues (Epstein, 1969), but further clarification of the substantive components of BGR is needed. For example, some studies may examine the attitudes of private sector executives toward government, or provide episodic public managerial perspectives, but the approach followed in this book attempts to integrate private and public sector managerial views on BGR using a common "real world" experience.

BACKGROUND AND CONTEMPORARY ISSUES

The 1980s has been a period of rethinking and introspection concerning American BGR. All kinds of examples point to a reconsideration of the appropriate interaction between America's two most powerful societal institutions—business and government.

Some of the questions that we ask and attempt to answer in this book are, "Where do we stand now?" and "What are the substantive issues in BGR?" Given progression of the events and discussion in the first half of the 1980s, our approach is to expand on the empirical and research knowledge base using data from informed private and public sector managers: we have examined current experienced-based, managerial attitudes toward American BGR. One specific objective is to use a data-based analytical perspective to meet the objectives of the book.

In the scholarly literature and through the work of pollsters, there have been presented results from an ample number of surveys about what the general population of private sector managers believe in reference to American BGR. Typical conclusions from such studies include observations similar to the following:

> Businessmen ... view government agencies as obstacles, constraints, delayers and impediments to economic progress. (Jacoby, 1975, p. 167)

> [Private sector managers] clearly felt that their counterparts [in the public sector] have more room for improvement than they do. (Driscoll, Cowger, and Egan, 1979, p. 54)

> Most executives ... feel that less government regulation of business is good for the country ... [and] that the federal government ought to be cut back radically. They believe government is by definition inefficient and are intrigued by the idea of turning over more government services to the private sector. (Moore, 1985, p. 75)

The themes implicit in these works are consistent with an adversarial model of American BGR that many have observed as the tradition and current exemplar in our society (e.g., Galbraith, 1973; Friedman and Friedman, 1979; McCraw, 1984). The themes are also consistent with the negativism toward government that characterized the "Reagan Revolution" of the 1980s.

As a counterpoint to the above, Levitt (1968) believes that the reflexive resistance to government is dangerous because business alienates its own "market." Levitt recounts the losing record of business in such social legislation matters as antitrust, trade, child labor, securities exchange, fair labor, housing, old-age survivors' insurance, education, and poverty. Levitt further argues that certain reforms actually benefited business and that it was clearly better off with the dissolution of giant trusts; national parks; elimination of child labor; legitimate labor unions; disclosure and regulation of securities; pure food and drug legislation; and highway/urban beautification. A critical remaining issue for society is whether business and public managers can overcome the historical and current myths and obstacles that have been stumbling blocks to effective BGR.

The research literature and popular business media dutifully suggest that further steps must be taken to alleviate the apparent lack of understanding between governmental and private executives. Because the interdependence between business and government is evident in issues of taxation, de-/reregulation, social equity, corporate bailouts, industrial policy debates, corporate fraud in government contracting, international trade/restrictions, and "business-like" approaches to government (e.g., Grace Commission), many have identified BGR as the *major* element in the study of business and society (Buchholz, 1980; Jones, 1983). Bok (1980) recognized the extensive and intensive nature of BGR interactions; astute practitioners such as Harold Geneen (1984) highlighted the need for contemporary, comprehensive approaches to BGR; and Wood (1985) described the utilitarian aspects of the cooperation-adversarial dualism in BGR. Mitnick (1980) comprehensively outlined the basic conceptual models that underlie regulation; Preston and Post (1975) and Preston (1980) examined the complexity of the public policy process and proposed a systematic "interpenetrating system" model. Others have presented relevant background and descriptive efforts in the study of BGR (e.g., Jacoby, 1975; Weidenbaum, 1977; Hughes, 1977; McGraw, 1984; Hurst, 1970; and Fox, 1982). However, the preponderance of current evidence supports the recent assessment by Steiner and Steiner (1985)—that no consensus or acceptable theory of BGR exists. This is especially perplexing given the increasing attention and important impacts of ineffective, conflictual approaches to public-private accommodation.

BUSINESS-GOVERNMENT RELATIONS
INTERORGANIZATIONAL STRATEGIES AND RESOURCE
DEPENDENCE

Generally, the traditional approach to BGR tends to be dichotomous, polarizing in effect, and posits either cooperative or adversarial approaches as explanations for behavior (e.g., see Jacoby, 1975). In reality, the relationships are most likely to be understood using a more flexible, contingency-based framework that represents an evolving continuum of BGR interactions, rather than a dichotomy of cooperation or conflict. That is, there is likely to be some form of cooperation or adversariness in most interactions between business and government, rather than only pure forms of collaboration or conflict. Defining the endpoints of the cooperation-conflict continuum is not critical for the purposes of this book, but the effects of this open system assumption are evident, and have multiple implications in terms of expected payoffs. In examining the traditional and emerging assumptions concerning the relationships between the private and public sectors, little empirical support for any model exists.

One relevant contemporary, conceptual approach that has both practical and theoretical merit for understanding BGR was proposed by Thompson and McEwen (1958). They classified certain broad interaction or interorganizational strategies as primarily either competitive or cooperative, but with each strategy exhibiting subcategories. According to Thompson and McEwen (1958), competition implies a complicated rivalry, probably for resources, between two or more organizations. Bargaining refers to the negotiation of an agreement for the exchange of goods or services between two or more organizations, or in this discussion the government and corporations. Co-optation was defined as the absorption of new elements into the leadership, decision-making, or policy-determining structure of an organization as a means of averting or "co-opting" threats (Thompson and McEwen, 1958). A coalition was described as a conscious combination of two or more organizations, possibly somewhat at cross purposes, to achieve a common purpose. Bargaining, co-optation, and coalition formation represent specific permutations of a general cooperative strategy in which resources are shared, rather than a conflicting or adversarial relationship that implies a zero sum posture with regard to resources. The adherence to or results of these intersectoral (public-private) or interorganizational strategies have short- and long-term implications for both business and government organizations or managers.

This conceptual framework is especially relevant to BGR in the context of external, uncontrollable forces such as the internationalization of trade, comparative, national economic strengths, and reliance on common energy and human resources. Cooperative strategies require an adaptive, flexible posture that explicitly or implicitly recognizes the role of scarce resources for mutual survival, whereas the calculus of competition or conflict does not explicitly recognize the systemic, resource, and future costs of adversarial relationships. This summary of potential interorganizational or intersector strategies in no way implies the existence of unidimensional models, or that the adversarial model is not effective in certain settings in which value questions may be contested. However, the approach does inquire as to the efficiency and interdependence effects of competition if effective use of resources is a legitimate systemwide criterion to gauge efficacious behavior.

Building on prior practical needs and conceptualizations, more recent open systems models of organization or management correctly emphasize the centrality of resource dependence and the influence of environmental or efficiency demands, which may be characterized as contingencies (e.g., Pfeffer and Salancik, 1978; Provan et al., 1980; Provan, 1984; and Preston, 1980). These approaches are referred to as system, efficiency, resource-dependence, agency, exchange, transaction, population ecology, or contingency theories because they emphasize the importance of transactions, efficiency, and external influences or resources as environmental variables in relationships between organizations or other institutional entities. As an example, one premise of the resource dependence perspective assumes that organizations are dependent, to varying degrees, on other organizations or identifiable environmental components for reducing uncertainty or acquiring scarce resources. Some organizations enter into inter-organizational or intersectoral relationships because they are de-pendent on other organizations, and desire to develop efficient and effective coping strategies for acquiring or efficiently allo-cating resources.

One example of this relationship may be that corporations or businesses incur resource costs to the extent that they either cooperate or compete with government organizations. Therefore, some managerial strategy or approach is needed to reduce loss of resources to either or both actors in the relationship. If business is highly dependent on resources (increased profit, return on investment, return to the shareholder, return on capital, etc.) that are mediated by government (e.g., regulations that require ex-penditures on safety equipment or pollution control), then man-agers may want to develop strategies that reduce the resource cost of governmental intervention. An interorganizational or managerial strategy to deal with government may then devise either cooperative, conflictual, competitive, or adversarial com-ponents based on the perception of how organizational resources will be best conserved, acquired, or expanded in the transaction.

Government regulators or other public agencies may, as con-trollers in the environment of business seeking to further public ends, directly affect the costs of private sector production, thereby reducing profit, return on investment, return on assets, or return to the shareholders or other stakeholders. Business or-ganizations, on the other hand, produce directly tangible eco-nomic benefits for the society and government indirectly through value added to products or services, wages, or taxes on corporate earnings. Business, society, and government organizations may incur unacceptable resource losses if productive business orga-nizations are overcontrolled or fail to provide adequate returns on the investments made in the firm. By itself, this argument does not naturally lead to the conclusion that cooperation or collaboration is always beneficial for either the public or the private sector. Evidence is mounting that highly coordinated or centralized economies may not be resource effective in the long term even though some shorter-term gains or contemporary ex-amples like Japan or Germany suggest that high levels or coop-eration or mutual planning may have benefits. Overall, resource dependence and interorganizational relations concepts (Pfeffer and Salancik, 1978; Van de Ven and Walker, 1984; Provan et al., 1980; and Provan, 1984) suggest that key external and internal resource-dependence issues will influence the effective level of BGR, intersectoral coordination, competition, or cooperation.

APPROACH TAKEN IN THIS BOOK

A central need for the study of interdependence between business and government is anchored in the practical and conceptual framework dilemmas. One requirement is for theoretical and empirical referents to address this interdependence systematically. The pragmatic need is to address real world relationships or issues in the most parsimonious way. To meet these sometimes competing needs, one objective of this book is to build on the fragmented foundations provided by relevant BGR literature. In addition, resource dependence and certain organizational theory concepts are used to understand business government interactions from the public sector and private sector managers' perspective. Figure 1–1 provides the general overview of some of the premises used in this book and study.

Because there is a relative lack of consensus concerning practical, theoretical, or empirical foundations on which to build, the approach used here examines questions that integrate propositions from resource-dependence, interorganizational, and BGR literature. The underlying premise in the general design is that BGR are pertinent to resource-dependence and system issues in the overall environmental context. The basic theoretical and practical argument is that interorganizational or intersectoral relationships will be associated with mutual strategies and resource dependence as perceived by the private sector and public sector managers being studied here. That is, if there are high perceived levels of resource dependence, then interorganizational strategies or BGR will be affected.

Figure 1–1 attempts to recognize that the public and private managers operate in separate task environments with different external and internal imperatives. Internal imperatives emanate from the tasks of maximizing return to the shareholder, profit, return on investment, and/or possibly even maximizing personal return or wealth. A composite theory of stakeholder management

Figure 1–1
Business-Government Interdependence Framework

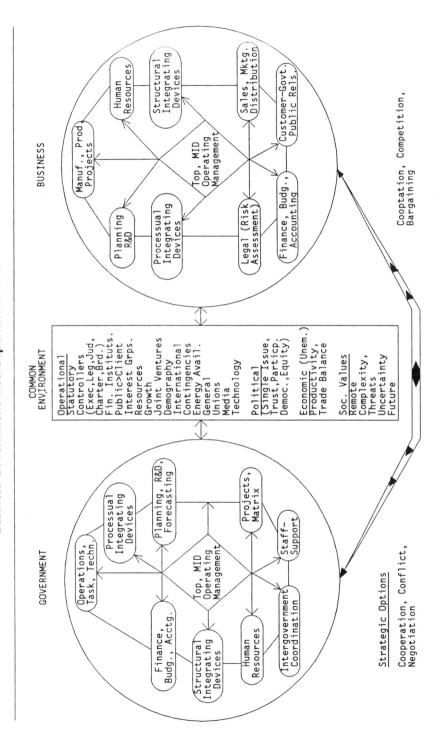

is not readily codified into operational definitions because of the competing, multiobjective, multiple constituent environment in which most nontrivial corporations or public organizations find themselves. This environment includes domestic, industrial, and international competitors that influence the private sector manager and governments to varying extents. There are also fluctuation levels of uncertainty and risk as well as political, economic, technological, legal, and other "market" influences that affect managerial perceptions and strategies. These strategies include developing long- and short-term resource allocation mechanisms to both internal and external functions.

A strategic management, market, or portfolio analysis that emphasizes industry, corporate, and business unit strengths, weaknesses, opportunities, and threats must align internal resources and functions with strategic objectives. Financial, temporal, human, structural, and information resources have to be systematically arrayed and designed to meet major or dominant competitive forces. These dominant competitive foci can be domestic and/or international in scope. An emergent premise is that government is a major buyer, supplier, or regulator that has significant resource implications, especially in the current era of global and past industrial transitions. The specific task environment, corporate, or business strategies should address business relationships with relevant government influences. A comprehensive strategy should exist because there are multiple potential linkages across common political, economic, international, legal, or technological dimensions where significant levels of interdependence may exist.

Complementing, opposing, accepting, or at least matching the managerial actions of private sector executives are the responsibilities and managerial strategies of public sector executives, whose responsibilities are primarily defined in statute and legislation. Any private sector action potentially affects the public, or specific segments, which brings oversight, control, adjudication, taxation, or regulation functions into play. Public managers are charged with formulating administrative procedures, strategies, or structures in meeting their statutory responsibilities.

As dominant consumers or clients of each other's products or outputs, business and government activities continuously intersect and converge. Yet few models have been used to explain or

shape these intersections. Figure 1–1 recognizes the task sepa-
rateness as well as the common "public" dimensions of both
public and private organizational/managerial activities. Each sector requires the other to behave responsibly in the "market" and
preferably in the common interest. One requirement is that mechanisms also have to be developed if the mutual actions are not
mutually beneficial or at least satisfactory. Private sector organizations and managers are major stakeholders in the environment of the public manager. Conversely, governmental and
public managerial functions are direct controllers, regulators,
clients, or adjudicators of private sector activities.

Figure 1–1 attempts to depict these manifold relationships in
an open system context in which each sector is directly dependent on and affected by the other, but within an atmosphere of
ambiguity, and/or conceptual or operational uncertainty. One
approach for redressing this long-standing imbalance is to con-
temporaneously reformulate the problem of BGR in a practical
setting, using pragmatic and conceptual analytical tools.

This book uses the basic propositions inherent in Figure 1–1,
the BGR literature, practical BGR dilemmas, and the resource-
relevant concepts discussed earlier to design a study of the attitudes and perceptions of top-level private sector and public
sector executives who cooperated in a one-state, public-private
partnership effort to improve state productivity.

GOVERNOR'S MANAGEMENT IMPROVEMENT
PROGRAM—A BUSINESSMAN WITH A BUSINESS PLAN?

Dolan (1984) provides an overview of the political, managerial,
and historical context for past efforts to unite business and government to improve government in New Jersey, where this study
is based. Traditional beliefs held in both the public and the business communities assumed that business executives could "right
the wrongs" of government. These Coolidgian beliefs have persisted to the present, where the Grace Commission, composed
of private sector executives, was the most current example of the
attitude that private sector managers are somehow more efficient
than public executives and are able to make government more

effective. The converse is rarely asserted or operationalized primarily because, according to private sector ideology, public managers never have to "make a profit" or "meet a payroll." Traditional antipathies and aphorisms abound in the area of BGR, but few have been systematically tested with mutually informed executives from both the private and the public sectors. As Dolan (1984) points out, the New Jersey State Archives were mute testimony to many past efforts that were read and buried.

Governor Thomas Kean, on June 29, 1982, created the Governor's Management Improvement Commission to undertake "the most comprehensive and far reaching analysis of state government ever attempted" (Dolan, 1984, p. 355). Three million dollars, thousands of hours, an 11-member Board of Directors, seven groups (with chair), and 30 individual teams of executives were formed to serve under the direction of the Governor's Management Improvement Program (GMIP). David R. Clare, president of Johnson and Johnson; Rocco J. Marano, then president of New Jersey Bell, and Robert R. Ferguson, Jr., president and chief executive officer of First National Bank Bancorp, constituted the core group that established this unprecedented effort of private executives and professional consultants to work with state government executives (Dolan, 1984). The GMIP focused on organizational structure and analysis, information systems analysis, cost avoidance, human service administration, program analysis, support services, staffing (including fringe benefits), long-term strategic issues, and the short-term objective of balancing the FY 1984 budget. One central aspect of the GMIP was that top-, mid-, and operational-level state agency executives acted as co-consultants, with several hundred leading New Jersey business and private sector managers included in the short-term process.

The joint cooperative GMIP was carefully designed from the beginning to avoid conflict of interest (i.e., private sector officials working with corresponding industry regulators). A unique facet of the program was that top- and mid-level managers in each of 20 state agencies had a parallel group of these private sector "co-consultants" to work with in examining and resolving major public management issues involved with efficiency, organizational structure, cost control, and information systems functions.

According to Dolan (1984), more than 250 private sector executives were involved at different levels in various coordinating or supporting roles in the joint cooperative project. Some of these

executives provided direct administrative support to the governing board, but did not have "hands-on" experience in the actual
management analysis, decision, or problem resolution phases of
the public agencies that were studied here. Of those who were
more or less directly involved in the overall project, there was
an effective group of approximately 168 private sector co-consultants, 78 of whom responded to a structured questionnaire.
Represented in the group of respondents were 18 presidents
(CEOs) or past presidents of major Fortune 500 and smaller corporations, 33 vice presidents from similar corporations, 18 assistant vice presidents and department heads, and 9 staff or
operations analysts. On the average, these corporate executives
had eight and one-half years' experience in their respective, most
recent positions and more than 26 years total in the private sector.
Taken together, these predominantly upper-level and operational
executives exhibited extensive corporate, professional, and BGR
experience. Given that similar studies have not been performed
with such a unique group of experienced executives, the potential for high levels of insight and explanation not found in previous studies is distinctive. The attitudes elicited from these
mutually informed executives go far beyond perceptions of either
"person in the street" or singular sector respondents.

Representing the public sector, there were 19 agency or de-
partmental secretaries, 46 deputy or assistant secretaries, 37 functional managers/heads, and 12 district managers or operations
analysts. The public executives, on the average, had more than
18 years in the public service and approximately 6 years in their
current positions. Taken together, these upper-level public and
private executives exhibited extensive managerial, corporate,
public service, professional, and BGR experience. This blend of
talent and experience forms a unique pool of knowledge and
perspectives relevant to the study of practical and conceptual
BGR issues. This intelligence was primarily focused on roles of
government and business, regulation, industrial policy, and BGR
strategies to build a common foundation of principles or understanding relevant to further conceptual development.

OVERVIEW

The individual chapters, analyses, and discussions address the
specific attitudes and perceptions of these public and private

executives in more detail. Chapter 2 focuses on the legal nature and premises of the adversarial relations between business and government. The regulatory dimension is the major focus, and it specifically examines the views of the public and private managers. Chapter 3 examines the relationships between resource dependence and BGR attitudes of the private sector executives to test the explanatory power of the two concepts as they relate to the underlying framework of this book.

Chapter 4 parallels and complements the study of resource dependence and BGR attitudes in Chapter 3 by analyzing only the perceptions of the public sector managers along the same dimensions as the private executives.

Chapter 5 uses a comparative bivariate approach to examine similar BGR attitudes across both groups of executives. Roles of business, government, regulation, industrial policy, and BGR are highlighted. Factor analyses are also used to test propositions that concern managerial accommodation in BGR.

Chapter 6 reviews and discusses the Grace Commission controversy as an example of contemporary, nonproductive government-business relations. Chapter 7 completes the book by examining the most relevant observations, findings, and conclusions from the study on which the book is based. The managerial and BGR research implications of the findings and related recommendations are also presented in Chapter 7. The Appendix contains the common instrument that was developed especially for the public and private managers who cooperated in this study.

CHAPTER 2

The Impact of Regulatory Cooperation on Business-Government Relations

It should be clear that information gathered *ex parte* from the public which become relevant to a rulemaking will have to be disclosed at some time. On the other hand, we recognize that informal contacts between the agencies and public are the "bread and butter" of the process of administration and are completely appropriate so long as they do not frustrate judicial review, or raise serious questions of fairness.

Home Box Office, Inc. *v.* FCC

Interactions between business and government are often adversarial. Many observers allege that inefficiency and mutual distrust result from this conflictual environment, thereby diverting resources away from more productive activities. The study in this chapter explores the regulatory dimension of business-government interdependence and the corresponding gap between the perceptions of business and government managers. One purpose of this approach is to attempt to develop the derivation of elements of an overall conceptual framework for more effective interaction. The application of certain elements of organizational theory is extended to interactions between business and government entities, to explore further the frontier of business-government relations (BGR).

ADVERSARIAL RELATIONS IN GOVERNMENT: THE JUDICIAL ANTECEDENTS

American law is derived from the British common law tradition that emphasizes adversarial conduct. The U.S. Constitution permits the expenditure of federal judicial resources only on "cases and controversies." This requires adversarial proceedings designed to create an atmosphere for the full presentation of facts and theoretical arguments. The premise is that the adversarial model pits opposing parties against each other who are fully motivated by the desire to win. According to supporters of this model, it naturally follows that the adversaries are more likely to marshal all resources at their disposal to win the dispute. This adversary model suggests that this kind of partisan opposition is most likely to yield sufficient information for accurate decision making.

In a nonadversarial or more cooperative context the incentives to ferret out accurate information or criticize inaccurate assertions supposedly are less intense. For example, when friendly parties are involved in judicial proceedings their arguments tend to be biased toward the mutual benefit of the cooperating parties. A general argument is that precedents set in such nonadversarial proceedings are less likely to represent the best interests of society than precedents set in an adversarial context. Instead, it is argued that disputes resolved in nonadversarial proceedings probably represent only the situation-specific best interest of the cooperating parties. Another supposition is that these cooperative outcomes are seldom sound bases for creating public policies that are set as precedents for later use. Adversarial theories suggest that the one-sided assertions of collaborators are seldom subjected to the rigors of cross-examination. Therefore, there is no accurate probing or testing of the assumptions or logic that underlies decisions concerning the contesting parties.

Many other areas of legal decision making also apply elements of the judicial adversarial model. The pervasiveness of this model is probably responsible for the general impression that few interactions between government and business are cooperative or beneficial for either party.

Despite the value of truth testing in the adversarial context, the system may lead to suboptimal resource allocation in some forms of conflict resolution. Litigation costs continue to rise, reflecting increasing legal fees, loss of productive time by litigants and witnesses, and long delays before final resolution. In order for courts to maintain their independent, objective role as impartial decision makers, the judiciary must attempt to maintain a certain distance from the dispute. For example, judges seldom have the responsibility to collect or probe information presented during trials. This duty primarily falls on the litigants. If the judiciary were solely responsible for all these probing tests, court costs would increase even more rapidly. Such a system would also bring into question the objectivity of the judiciary and the fairness of its decisions. Indeed, to complement the adversarial model and avoid the bias inherent in partisanship, the judiciary should refrain from participating in the advocacy needed for adequate adversarial relations. Therefore, supporters of the adversarial model argue that it is more efficient than other models of dispute-settling mechanisms, particularly when the opposing parties have strong contrary views about the facts, the public policies, to be applied, or face a zero-sum outcome.

In situations that involve the allocation of limited resources to competitors, an adversarial system may be the natural and possibly the inevitable result of interaction. If all parties cannot be fully satisfied from the stakes available, then there must necessarily be winners and losers. Many elements of the political and legal system exhibit the zero-sum characteristics of adversarial conflict. For example, political races for public office and referenda are nearly always fought in an adversarial manner. Prospective legislation is advocated and attacked by partisan adversaries who often perceive that they have diametrically opposing interests. Within this adversarial framework it is not surprising that regulatory agencies perceive their regulated entities to be adversaries and vice versa. Regulators often interpret their mission as one that requires oversight and policing activities. Regulatory agencies may execute their legislative, executive, and judicial functions in an adversarial manner similar to that of the surrounding political and legal system. They are often staffed by lawyers with experiences primarily from the adversarial litigation system.

REGULATION AND ADVERSARIAL RELATIONS

Interactions between business and government entities arise for many reasons and in many forms. The executive branch often investigates, prosecutes, or negotiates with businesses and its employees. Legislatures respond variously to business needs, to its lobbying, or to perceived abuses of the law and market failures. These responses usually create the structural forces leading to partisan controversy and often result in litigation by and against businesses.

Regulatory bodies have various missions that are determined by numerous influences. The enabling legislation establishes agencies and authorizes appropriate structures and operations. These agencies' missions are periodically reinterpreted by the executive branch, in response to public pressures, or even as a result of ideological evolution of the agencies' leaders. For example, legislators often create agencies or laws where abuses by businesses have occurred or have been perceived. Regulatory agencies naturally tend to oppose certain behaviors of citizens and businesses. However, there have also been examples of nurturing missions, as in agriculture and the early development of atomic energy. In the scheme of things the executive administration usually has ultimate control over regulatory agencies. This permits the president or governor or other chief executive to require certain levels of policy conformance by changing the agency's mission or some of its procedural elements. This also permits a pro-business chief executive to formulate broad policies to protect and nurture business, as opposed to a pro-consumer or pro-environment administration, which increases policing efforts. Activist courts also impose modification of the regulatory agency's mission in accordance with the court's interpretation of constitutional and statutory law. These various sources of regulatory mission, control, and policy create dilemmas for agency policymakers. However, there are increasing opportunities for changes in BGR, particularly as these missions are modified or numerous agencies are reorganized.

Most business and government managers believe that their relationship together is largely adversarial. Jacoby (1975) noted:

> Officials of government characteristically look upon themselves as probers, inspectors, taxers, regulators, and punishers of business transgressions. Businessmen typically view government agencies as obstacles, constraints, delayers, and impediments to economic progress.

Of course some exceptions have developed in certain narrower situations in which the parties may perceive a mutual advantage from their cooperation. When business and government goals converge, adversarial conduct often diminishes. These situations may arise when matters of national interest predominate, in relationships with foreign nations, or in competition with other governments. These situations permit a cooperative environment to arise, shifting the adversarial relationships between business and government.

Ultimately there are absolute political, economic, and practical constraints that prevent the assimilation of business into government or government into business. Despite the potential for societal contributions by business, there is widespread belief that business is always capable of some detrimental action. Similarly, experience with dictatorial governments suggests that government should not grow too large or dominate all aspects of life. Adversariness between the two institutions can provide extra-constitutional checks and balances on the abuse of power. Indeed, the United States Constitution was designed to prevent an excessively close partnership between business and government.

Some critics charge that business dominates government (Stone, 1975), whereas others complain that government dominates business (Friedman and Friedman, 1979). In addition, the "revolving door" concept suggests that employment in both business and government promotes a certain symbiosis (Galbraith, 1973). Given these strong pressures to maintain adversariness, one might conclude that cooperation is impossible. However, pressure is increasing to refine and reduce the cost of adversarial BGR.

CHARACTERISTICS OF BUSINESS-GOVERNMENT COOPERATION

Several strong and popular movements to reduce the costs of business-government adversariness are becoming evident. Pressure to deregulate has been strong throughout the 1970s and 1980s. There are also pressures on businesses to encourage deregulation by increasing their own social performance (Wartick and Cochran, 1985). Deregulation may be responsible for im-

proving the economic performance of society through the reduction of deficits, excessive taxation, and intrusion into
personal liberty. Societal resources may be efficiently used if
regulators consider technical feasibility, competitive pressures,
and the increased internationalization of competition. This regulatory dilemma inherently depends on business' avoidance of
regulatory burdens through responsible action. The pressures to
re-regulate are reinforced when businesses fail to consider the
impact of political reaction to business decisions. The political
response to perceived irresponsibility by business is often characterized by overreaction. For instance, a regulatory revival may
cause a severer impact on business than if careful initial planning
had been undertaken by business. Given these trends, an increase
in business-government cooperation appears to be more publicly
acceptable.

Adversary relations are most likely to occur when the opposing
parties compete for scarce resources or when a controversy will
result in discrete outcomes. The potential for win-win outcomes
in zero-sum BGR environments is limited. However, a resource
dependency model may be used to explain some behavior of
both business and government entities when they exhibit mutual
interdependence. For example, a regulated business and a particular regulatory agency may depend on each other for potential
resources. In such situations greater cooperation may increase
the success of both. For example, the Commerce Department
collects statistics from businesses that are important to the success of nearly all businesses. The licensing of nuclear power
plants or broadcasters also exhibits elements of mutual survival.
Some regulatory agencies provide technical assistance and resources to business in order to increase productivity. Examples
include the Small Business Administration and most state agricultural programs. These relationships illustrate the trust that
arises between business and government when there is a higher
correlation between their respective goals. Such environments
are most likely to yield cooperative interaction.

It is probably not conceptually useful in the area of regulation
to characterize BGR as completely adversarial and cooperative,
or the relationship between them as strictly dichotomous. The
placement of a particular regulatory program on an adversarial-
cooperative continuum depends on several factors. A particular

regulatory agency may have elements of both cooperation and adversariness in any of the many programs administered. In addition, over time the focus of a regulatory agency may change, and its policies may be revised to reflect the executive administration in power or the personal biases of agency personnel.

The factors important to characterizing relations between a particular agency and its regulated constituency depend on several conditions. First, the respective missions of the agency and the regulated entities may exacerbate the differences in goals. This situation creates a different imperative for the BGR interaction or interdependence. Second, the number and quality of interactions between the business and government agency should be considered. Increased cooperative quality and frequency of interaction will often lead to improved relations. That is, limited and extremely divisive contacts are harmful to cooperative relations. Third, the choice of methods to reduce inefficient or adversarial contacts is important. Finally, the attitudes of private sector and public sector personnel are important. Current attitudes may lead to future postures derived from past experiences.

The Federal Trade Commission (FTC) has long been considered a policing agency because it imposed its own views of "fair competition." The FTC's adversariness abruptly changed with the appointment of a strong free market economist as chairman in the early 1980s. Since that time the FTC has moved along the continuum from adversarial to "cooperative" relations. By contrast, with changes in leadership, the Securities and Exchange Commission (SEC) has moved from a cooperative posture to a more adversarial one in recent years. The appointment in the 1980s of SEC commissioners who believed in promoting a "fair market" has resulted in increased disclosure requirements and a stronger enforcement of the securities laws.

In the past, several methods to facilitate improvements in BGR have been attempted. First, cooperation is facilitated when business leaders and government policymakers understand each other's mission. Cooperation arises when mutual understanding, rather than mistrust, is at the root of the relationship. Second, when either entity accepts the justification for the opposition's goals, cooperation may be improved. Thus, acceptance of the other's legitimacy improves the adoption and similarity of both goals. Further, it may be possible for one side to co-opt the other into adopting each other's goals. Finally, cooperation is significantly enhanced when coalitions develop between regulators and regulated entities.

Co-optation depends on a congruence of attitudes between business and government managers. Mutual assimilation of goals and attitudes becomes more likely when each side gains a greater understanding of the other's mission and methods through various contacts. It might be hypothesized that the quality and frequency of these interactions are directly related to empathy and sympathetic understanding. When such interaction occurs, changes in attitudes may be measured, suggesting an improvement in the business-government atmosphere. However, such cooperative ventures must carefully adhere to several legal constraints on the process of cooperation. These constraints have been developed to avoid conflicts of interest and to maintain the checks and balances system. Careful adherence to existing legal constraints on cooperation should permit the construction of useful mechanisms to improve BGR.

LEGAL CONSTRAINTS ON COOPERATIVE BUSINESS GOVERNMENT RELATIONS

The constitutional concept of due process requires that impartial tribunals be available for resolution of disputes. This has led to the creation of an elaborate system of quasi-independent administrative law judges (ALJs) who are responsible for hearing disputes that arise from federal regulatory prosecutions. The decisions of ALJs are considered valid only when the judges are not biased in favor of either party. Biases may arise from a financial stake in an outcome, a personal conflict with the regulated entity, an overdependence on a particular political ideology, an economic theory, or political administration. Regulators must maintain independence and objectivity by refraining from receiving or initiating *ex parte contacts*. These contacts are often made off the record as oral or written communications between regulators and regulated parties. They can range from clearly illegal threats or bribes through well-meaning policy advocacy to helpful information. The prohibition against ex parte contacts is designed to preserve a fair and unbiased atmosphere when decisions are made between adversaries who probe the policy theories and factual evidence presented by the opposition.

A basic concept critical to the value of adversarial decision making is the constitutional concept of *confrontation*. The Sixth Amendment to the United States Constitution has been interpreted to prohibit ex parte contacts made between either regulators or regulated entities and the ALJs if they are involved in litigation. If ex parte contacts are made by one party but the opposing party is ignorant of the contact, it may become impossible for the ignorant party to effectively confront the matter discussed. The quality of all the information presented is thereby compromised. When the ALJ relies on information not fully tested by confrontation (e.g., cross-examination), then unfair or suboptimal decisions may be reached. In addition, it becomes impossible to accurately appeal a ruling made by an ALJ who was influenced by unconfronted ex parte contacts. Extensive ex parte contacts prevent the appeals court from identifying the basis of the original decision when the contacts are not made part of the official administrative record.

In recent years the courts have extended the ex parte contact prohibition beyond formal adjudications made by ALJs. In some instances off-the-record contacts with regulators in informal proceedings have also been prohibited. For example, regulations are promulgated at the discretion of regulators in the "notice and comment" rule-making procedures. Agency personnel examine the formal record for comments from regulated entities and from other affected parties. This is an important source of information concerning the advisability and impact of proposed new rules. Interested parties are directed to enter their comments only on the official record. Therefore, any statement asserted as fact or as theory determinative of results expected from the proposed regulations are exposed to confrontation by any interested parties. However, full trial-like procedures are usually considered too costly in rule-making proceedings. The facts presented are usually more general or are scientifically based; they are considered *legislative facts*. The reliability of legislative facts is seldom improved through cross-examination. Only the quality of *adjudicatory fact* determinations is improved with cross-examination. These facts concern past discrete events and are afforded the trial-like opportunity for confrontation and cross-examination. The memory and bias of potentially interested parties and witnesses are probed only in adjudicatory settings where adjudicatory facts are at issue.

There is a complicating factor in cooperative BGR, from some conflicting decisions in the federal courts about the extent of the ex parte contact prohibition. In one case the HBO cable network challenged the Federal Communications Commission (FCC) in a rule-making proceeding. The FCC promulgated a rule that restricted the exhibition of feature films and sports events (Home Box Office, Inc. v. FCC, 1977). The FCC had a procedural rule that prohibited public comments made to the Commission after the last day of testimony. However, in this instance the FCC was contacted by nearly every interested party after the prohibition became effective. The court of appeals concluded that these ex parte contacts tainted the rule making because the comments were not entered into the official record. This limited the accuracy of judicial review when appeal was made.

Later the same year the same United States Court of Appeals made a turnabout by refusing to apply the ex parte contact rule in another FCC rule making (Action for Children's Television v. FCC, 1977). The FCC had responded to a public request to restrict certain advertising techniques because they were unfair. For example, the FCC proposed to restrict advertising directed to children that used cartoon heroes, to restrict commercials that depicted dangerous activities not in compliance with safety regulations, to clearly separate program content from advertising, and to eliminate certain deceptive sales practices. However, the FCC declined to impose the proposed rule, and instead coerced the National Association of Broadcasters (NAB) into adopting changes in the television code through a jawboning process. The television code is a form of private regulation voluntarily observed by all broadcasters. The jawboning process, in this case, was considered "impolitic" but not illegal by the court of appeals. Ex parte contacts were permissible because there were no "competing claims" to a valuable privilege. The FCC successfully used the same off-the-record jawboning process to eliminate sex and violence on broadcast television during the "family viewing hour" (Writer's Guild of America v. FCC, 1976).

In summary, it would appear that some ex parte contacts are

becoming more acceptable if compliance with safeguards is required for informal adjudications. However, in designing joint business-government cooperation programs or efforts, great care must be taken to avoid any appearance that ex parte contacts are likely.

JOINT GOVERNMENT IMPROVEMENT PROGRAMS

Several programs with different thrusts have recently been initiated to improve government efficiency. For example, the Grace Commission appears to have been developed using the inquisition model. This type of program is based on the assumption that governmental agency personnel possess inadequate managerial talents, easily yield to conflicts of interest, or act only to preserve their own employment. The recommendations of Grace-type commissions often call for the elimination of programs and allege regulator deficiencies. However, these conflictual approaches are often based on fundamental disagreements or misperceptions about the mission of the regulatory agencies and not on the allegedly poor managerial performance of regulators. These programs are often conducted with an air of superiority and contempt for regulatory agency personnel and their methods. It inevitably engenders resentment and resistance by the government personnel. The recommendations of Grace-type commission reports are usually contrary to basic agency goals as stated in their enabling legislation. With this type of approach and underlying biases, not to mention poor outcomes, it seems prudent to explore other means to achieve government efficiency or improvement in BGR.

In contrast to adversarial business-government improvement projects, a few examples of voluntary and cooperative projects have arisen. These are premised on the recognition that there is some measure of similarity or mutuality in goals between the business and government units involved. Such projects may necessitate voluntary participation by all parties involved, rather than conflict. For example, federal environmental officials, state environmental regulators, coal producers, and environmental interest groups joined together in the National Coal Policy Project to work out the reclamation of stripped mined land (Gray and

Hay, 1985). In another example recent efforts by the SEC, the Department of Justice, the New York Stock Exchange, and several brokerage firms assisted in the identification and prosecution of inside traders. These examples illustrate that when business and government share similar goals, a voluntary cooperative project that benefits the system as a whole is more likely.

Certain state government improvement projects have also used a cooperative approach. In reducing the inquisition-like character or procedures, it is more likely that regulators will participate and believe in the value of the recommendations, thereby improving the chances of longer-term results and efficiencies. In these types of programs the business and government participants have adopted a cooperative goal of improving the efficiency of government operations. Such cooperation is more likely to lead to permanent changes in work patterns. However, there is still potential for conflict of interest, bias, and undue influence whenever regulators and the regulated entities interact extensively outside their normal relationships. It becomes imperative to avoid the appearance of illegal or even unsavory ex parte contacts in the design of such government improvement programs. This chapter examines the private sector and public sector managerial attitudes toward regulation to develop a more refined understanding of the BGR-regulation issues. The legality of contacts between regulators and their regulated entities was explicitly recognized in this approach.

The designers of the New Jersey Governor's Management Improvement Program (GMIP) being studied here were careful to avoid allegations of ex parte contacts. The various working groups of nearly 400 managers were designed to avert the appearance or possibility of ex parte contacts. No group assignments matched regulators with executives from the industries directly regulated. Therefore, a sound basis for independence was formally established into the cooperative program structure.

Part of the GMIP study focused on approximately 16 regulatory items selected from the 80 normative descriptive statements, which were used to examine attitudes. These regulatory questions were assessed using a 5-point Likert scale anchored by strong disagreement (1) and strong agreement (5). Responses to the regulatory items from both the public sector and the private sector groups were compared using t tests. Table 2–1 summarizes the response means and standard deviations and the cumulative response percentages of both groups for these items (see Appendix A). The implications of these results are discussed next.

RESULTS AND DISCUSSIONS

The analyses and results of the two sets of responses to the regulatory questions provide several interesting attitudinal patterns. The private sector executives are contrasted with the public sector executives. In the following discussion three concepts developed earlier are examined in relation to the responses of the two groups. These concepts include cooperation, adversariness, and the avoidance of illegal conflicts of interest (ex parte contacts). The discussion is classified roughly into three areas: (1) the identification of regulatory concerns, (2) communication between regulators and business executives concerning regulatory policies, and (3) business' impact on regulatory proposals.

Identification of Regulatory Concern

Both business and public executives perceived that trade associations are the most regularly used source for identification of regulatory concerns for business. In-house legal counsel is perceived by both groups to be the next most often used source for identification of regulatory concerns. The third major source of information includes both outside legal counsel and consultants. These were followed by personal review of government documents by business executives.

The government documents most often used are the official and primary compendiums of regulators' intentions, expectations, and decisions. They include such regularly published documents as the *Federal Register* and the biannual *Regulatory Agendas*. These documents permit the identification of rule proposals, determinations by agencies, and certain policy conclusions leading to rules and determinations. Many state governments issue similar documents and special reports, but the information is often poorly organized and not widely distributed. Many government documents are published by various

Table 2–1
Sample from Questionnaire on Business-Government Relations

PROPOSITION

Business Impact on Regulatory Concerns Variables

Business affected by regulation appears to take every legitimate opportunity to assist in the formulation of regulatory policy.

Business has many opportunities to present views to regulators on specific regulatory proposals.

Business regularly presents its views to regulators on particular regulatory proposals.

Business estimates of the expected costs and benefits of regulatory proposals underlie business' support or opposition of the proposals.

Business economic analyses of regulatory proposals are regularly provided to regulators to assist in the efficient selection of regulatory actions.

The concerns of business are most often accepted by public policy makers in the regulatory policy finally adopted.

Alternatives to achieve deregulation should be considered as a major objective by government agencies.

Government regulations should include provisions that require business and government to develop cooperative approaches for meeting regulatory objectives.

Policy Communication Variables

Business should attempt to assist in the formulation of regulatory policies through dialogue with the executive branch (e.g., governor, president, cabinet).

Business should attempt to assist in the formulation of regulatory policies through dialogue with legislators to shape administrative agency powers.

Business should attempt to assist in the formulation of regulatory policies through direct contacts with the relevant administrative agency.

Regulatory Concern Identification Variables

The process of identifying and assessing the impact of regulatory action or proposals involves the collaboration of management with legal counsel.

Business identifies potential areas of regulatory concern by: reading regularly published government documents;

. . .by: being alerted by in-house legal counsel;

. . .by: being alerted by outside consultants or law firms;

. . .by: trade associations.

28

Table 2-1 (continued)

| PRIVATE SECTOR | | | | | PUBLIC SECTOR | | | | |
| Summary Statistics | | Cumulative Response Percentages | | | Cumulative Response Percentages | | | Summary Statistics | |
Response Mean	Std. Dev.	Disagree	Neutral	Agree	Disagree	Neutral	Agree	Response Mean	Std. Dev.
3.195	1.077	35.1	13	52	22.9	15.8	61.4	3.491	1.015
3.571	.751	11.7	23.4	64.9	4.5	13.6	81.7	3.9	.741
3.532	.771	14.3	20.8	64.9	10.7	11.6	77.7	3.831	.811
3.707	.731	8	17.3	74.6	5.6	14.8	79.6	3.861	.69
2.948	.916	35.1	36.4	28.6	29.7	30.6	39.6	3.117	.922
2.649	.823	49.4	32.5	18.2	22.2	40.7	37.1	3.167	.791
3.697	.895	13.1	15.8	71.1	20.2	18.3	61.4	3.477	.919
3.468	1.046	18.2	24.7	57.2	11.4	15.8	72.8	3.711	.859
4.065	.656	3.9	2.6	93.5	4.4	3.5	92.1	4.009	.634
4.182	.556	1.3	3.9	94.8	5.3	5.3	89.4	3.991	.726
4.143	.683	2.6	9.1	88.3	6.2	4.4	89.4	4.018	.732
3.597	.921	15.6	15.6	68.8	3.5	23.7	72.8	3.746	.607
3.584	.918	15.6	15.6	68.8	10.5	21.9	67.5	3.649	.776
3.857	.756	6.5	13	80.5	6.1	21.1	72.8	3.754	.698
3.727	.737	7.8	16.9	75.3	6.1	25.4	68.4	3.693	.693
3.987	.573	2.6	9.1	88.3	.9	14.9	83.4	4.026	.658

government printing offices and then republished by private loose-leaf services (e.g., Commerce Clearing House). Most in-house and outside consultants who provide regulatory concern information utilize these same documents.

Curiously, business executives rely on other personnel to examine these documents rather than use their own direct personal examination. One might hypothesize that executives consider these documents to be specialized or esoteric legal documents, and that it is more efficient for specialists who are more familiar with their format and technical features to review them first. However, it would appear more appropriate for business executives to become more directly involved with the analysis of government documents. Regular examination of these documents and more accurate interaction with regulators would probably lead to earlier detection of issues and greater understanding by both business executives and regulators. Continued reliance on legal counsel or consultants to identify regulatory concerns suggests that adversarial relations will continue. Another explanation might be that executives look to legal counsel when regulation involves resource implications or they perceive serious potential adversariness. Business executives are probably better suited to identification of regulatory concerns because of their substantive understanding of the business matters regulated.

Regulators perceive that business executives are alerted to regulatory concerns by trade associations and government document examination more than the executives believe this. By contrast, executives believe that in-house and outside legal counsel and consultants are responsible for identification of regulatory concerns more so than the regulators. These discrepancies may also be explained by the adversarial hypothesis. Legal counsel detect and focus on adversarial relationships because of a preoccupation with that form of interaction. Apparently regulators perceive that the growth in participation by trade associations and business executives is becoming more significant as a method for identifying regulatory concerns than reliance on legal counsel. This might be explained by two factors. First, legal counsel has historically had general access to regulatory documents yet seldom becomes directly involved with regulators unless litigation arises. Second, trade associations may be perceived more as lobbying organizations, with a corresponding higher visibility to regulators than is the profile of in-house counsel.

The results of the questions that show business executives' attitudes about legal counsel may be somewhat inconsistent with the executives' general perception that a lesser role exists for legal counsel compared with the regulator's perception of this role. The traditional tension between executives and legal counsel could account for some of this disparity. Business executives probably know the regularity and reliability of their sources for regulatory alert better than do outsiders, such as regulators. These results suggest that regulators may have underestimated the importance of private legal counsel in the regulatory scanning process. In addition, lawyers are probably more careful to avoid the appearance of having ex parte contacts directly with regulators than are business executives or trade associations. Lawyers may be familiar with conflict of interest laws. It is also possible that business executives are not taking full advantage of their access to regulators made through trade associations.

Communication of Policy Matters

Both business executives and the regulators generally agree that dialogue between them occurs quite frequently. Both groups feel strongly that direct communication is appropriate for setting regulatory policy. Direct communication between business executives, and legislators, regulators, and the executive branch is perceived as appropriate, despite the ex parte contact rule. Given the prevalence of this attitude, legal counsel for both business and government executives should more carefully determine whether direct communications will be entered on the public record. When such communications are entered on the regulatory record, both parties may need to rethink the type of subjects discussed and the details communicated. Both groups have favorable views of communication as a basis for cooperation. This also suggests that cooperative BGR, such as the improvement program studied here, hold promise for developing a more cooperative atmosphere.

Impact of Business on Regulatory Proposals

The results indicate that regulators believe that business takes more initiative in the formulation of regulatory policies than business executives believe it does. Regulators also believe that business has more opportunities to affect public policy than business executives believe. These observations are consistent with business executives' closer contact with their own sources of regulatory scanning. That is, the regulators' perception of greater business impact on policy might be explained by the regulators' immersion into deregulation, regulatory impact analyses and cost-benefit/analyses, and the actual machinery of regulatory process (e.g., rule-making, adjudication, and policy-setting processes). These multiple processes may give them the impression of extensive influence by business. Most business executives are more concerned with their own operational problems than with those of the regulators. The results show that both groups recognize that business fails to take advantage of all its legitimate opportunities to affect regulatory policy. This implies some support for the descriptive power of the adversarial model of regulatory process. It also appears that both groups could benefit from participation in more cooperative regulatory processes.

Other results show that both business and regulators have the opportunity to conduct cost-benefit/analysis (C-B/A) to evaluate the impact of particular regulatory proposals. Both regulators and business executives believe that these regulatory impact analyses (C-B/A's) are conducted by business on a regular basis. The conduct of more economic impact analyses by businesses and regulators is more likely to reduce the cost of regulations on society. By this process both sides may confront the assumptions, hypotheses, and computations used to justify new regulations. At the federal government level, all "major rules" that have a significant economic impact must be subjected to regulatory impact analysis (C-B/A). This process was initiated by President Ford to reflect the inflation impact of regulations, raised to a formal C-B/A under President Carter, and ultimately mandated in 1981 for all department-level federal agencies by President Reagan in Executive Order No. 12,291.

Business executives and regulators show some disagreement as to the actual use of economic impact analyses of regulations. First, regulators perceive that business conducts C-B/A's more often than business executives think it does. Second, both groups believe that C-B/A's are not submitted to regulators as often as businesses prepare them. This suggests that a disparity exists between preparation and presentation of *quantitative C-B/A*, and the *qualitative* presentation of general views on regulatory proposals. It may also suggest that businesses prepare C-B/A's but withhold them from regulators on some occasions. Perhaps business perceives that the C-B/A results are not helpful to its position in certain instances. It might also be hypothesized that business executives perceive that some C-B/A's are inconclusive, susceptible to misinterpretation, or even damaging to business' position on some regulatory proposals.

On first examination, the presentation of business' C-B/A's to regulators would appear to support the cooperative model. However, when the use of C-B/A is intended to correct or stand in contrast to the regulators' computation of C-B/A, then the process appears more likely to be adversarial. An alternative hypothesis states that C-B/A's may be perceived by both regulators and business as being too complex, or are submitted excessively late to be useful in regulatory policymaking. Business may also withhold its C-B/A's if convinced that rhetoric, jawboning, political pressure, or public sympathy is more effective to formulate regulatory policies. The trend in federal rule making is to enter all C-B/A's onto the public record. This nearly assures public scrutiny of the cost and benefit estimates, particularly when the ex parte contact rule deters off-the-record communications.

Successful businesses have extensive experience in the preparation of economic analyses. It would appear that business could take greater advantage of this experience to shape regulatory policies. Indeed, there is an opportunity to gain widespread respect by regulators and the public if business prepares C-B/A's in good faith and with reasonable assumptions. The appearance that C-B/A's are more or less objective and not partisan or adversarial would be likely to improve the perception that business is cooperating. C-B/A's prepared at the federal level are not reviewable by courts of law. When the validity of new regulations or their propriety are attacked in litigation, the C-B/A's used to justify the rules may not be questioned on appeal. There is little risk for business or regulators who prepare C-B/A's in good faith.

Business Impact

In the business impact results there are fundamental disagreements between the attitudes of business executives and regulators concerning the practical impact that business may have on setting regulatory policies. Regulators believe that business views are assimilated into regulatory policies to a much greater extent than business executives believe they are. Half of the business executives surveyed disagree with the proposition that their communications impact on regulatory outcomes to any real extent. This is consistent with the hypotheses that a mutual, fundamental adversarial posture currently exists between regulators and businesses. By contrast, the regulators perceive that business impact on the regulatory process is much greater. Business executives' general perception of helplessness is somewhat inconsistent with the level of effort they undertake to change regulatory policies. If business executives truly believe that they have little impact on regulatory outcome, then perhaps they are wasting resources in their regulatory interactions. However, it is more plausible that businesses are not always successful in averting regulations perceived as costly. Therefore, business executives may underestimate the usefulness of their efforts. This also supports the adversariness hypothesis, and suggests that business executives fundamentally view their relationship with regulators as adversarial. It also suggests that business executives ignore the regulators' public interest mission as required by statute. Both groups of executives perceive that regulatory alternatives should be generated in an effort to achieve more deregulation. Predictably, regulators are somewhat less receptive to generating alternatives than are business executives. Clearly, deregulation is a more fundamental objective for business executives than for regulators. This disparity may reflect the political popularity of deregulation. Regulators are sympathetic to adoption of statutory enforcement procedures to require cooperative approaches to meet regulatory objectives. Business executives may be in a better position to identify the difficulties of making changes in business practice required by new regulations. However, the adversariness ethic appears quite entrenched and suggests the difficulties of gaining widespread BGR cooperation.

CONCLUDING COMMENTS

Results from analyzing the regulatory questions by this questionnaire suggest that exposure to cooperative nonadversarial relations lead to some attitude changes by private sector executives. For example, most private sector executives are impressed with the amount and quality of work performed by regulators. However, there may be limitations to these attitudinal changes (i.e., the benefits of business-government cooperation may not be long lasting). Informal interviews with some respondents reveal some skepticism about whether these attitude changes are temporary, unless regular follow-up efforts are undertaken to reinforce them. First, public sector and private sector managers who are not involved in the program are unlikely to experience the same attitude change. Second, repetition of these cooperative programs may be necessary so that executives are reminded of their experiences and are reinforced. It might be argued that business-government relation improvement programs should be conducted at regular intervals. This would refamiliarize the parties with the insights provided by the program. In addition, those managers who participate in cooperative programs should share their experiences with nonparticipating co-workers.

The study results in this chapter present additional evidence that the adversarial context may be considered necessary by business and inevitable in situations where scarce resources are allocated or a zero-sum outcome is certain. However, in most other contexts an increase in well-meaning contacts between regulators and regulated entities could yield more efficient results. To be effective, cooperative contacts must be carefully designed to avoid violation of the ex parte contact prohibition. There may also be a need to enter these contacts on the official record. The advantages of cooperative business-government relations may be limited until business understands the extent of initiative that it should take in dealing with legitimate societal problems when not forced to do so by government. In summary, it would appear that the legal context is no barrier to effective cooperation between business and government.

CHAPTER 3

Private Sector Managerial Attitudes in Business-Government Relations

> This evolutionary view of the business society, with its intertwined strands of enterprise, market economics, politics, and consensual social justice, is basic to any attempt to think toward "a positive image of the future." The positive image must begin with an appreciation of the intricately balanced system that combines a central political consensus with independent-minded, opportunity-oriented, profit-disciplined centers of development, production, and service, each interacting with the other.
>
> LOUIS BANKS
> "The Mission of Our Business Society"
> *Harvard Business Review*

As alluded to in Chapter 1, events in the 1980s led to considerable reconsideration of American business-government relations (BGR). The Chrysler "bailout" led to increased discussion of cooperative business-government programs. The threat from foreign producers prompted widespread debate about the need for a U.S. industrial policy. Deregulation was extended to suggest privatizing many traditionally public sector activities (e.g., postal services). The Grace Commission fueled ongoing arguments about waste in government spending. The chemical leaks at Bhopal, the "check-kiting" scheme by E. F. Hutton, insider trading on Wall Street, and corporate involvement in South Africa kept alive the questions of corporate social responsibility and corporate social performance. Thoughtful private sector managers have considered most of these matters and formed opinions. All of these events influence public, government, and corporate attitudes relating to the American business-government relationship.

The central questions in this chapter are (a) what are the major contemporary business-government issues, and (b) where do we stand in terms of developing explanatory frameworks for business-government relations using relevant concepts such as resource dependence. Given the events and discussion in the first half of the 1980s, what are informed private sector managers' attitudes toward American business-government relations and what are the implications of these attitudes for the 1990s and beyond?

BACKGROUND

Studies and analyses of American business-government relations have been conducted from a number of perspectives. Studies of the history of the relationships show that business and government have generally been adversaries in American society (McGraw, 1984), even though many have suggested that increased cooperation is needed (Jacoby, 1975). Some have argued that during the past few decades, government has dominated business (Friedman and Friedman, 1979; Hughes, 1977), but as well there are those who believe that business dominated government (Galbraith, 1973; Stone, 1975). Some analysts focus on the interaction of economic and political systems (Lindblom, 1977), whereas others look at issues that result from that interaction (Weidenbaum, 1977). Only on occasion, however, do studies of business-government relations focus on the roles and attitudes of the participants in the relationship (i.e., the public sector and private sector managers). With a few exceptions, looking at public sector and private sector managers' attitudes has been left to the pollsters, who have descriptive rather than analytical objectives in mind.

Among those few studies that have tried to look at public sector and/or private sector managers' attitudes toward business-government relations is a work that resulted from a 1974 seminar at the University of California at Los Angeles (UCLA). This study concluded that

> Officials of government characteristically look upon themselves as probers, inspectors, taxers, regulators and punishers of business transgressions. Businessmen typically view government agencies as obstacles, constraints, delayers and impediments to economic progress. (Jacoby, 1975, p. 167)

The adversariness apparent in this observation speaks for itself. An unfortunate consequence of such adversariness is that it leads to stereotyping and oversimplification—stereotyping of the "opposition" and oversimplification of methods for "winning the game."

To contend with these problems, increased cooperation is often suggested. To illustrate, consider a recent study of more than 100 public sector and private sector managers (Driscoll, Cowger, and Egan, 1979). A major finding of this study was that "each side clearly felt that their counterparts have more room for improvement than they do" (p. 54), even though in actuality there was little or no difference in their jobs. Specifically, private sector managers believed that they were under greater time pressures, responsibilities, and consumer demands than were public sector managers. Stereotyping was suggested as the key underlying cause of these perceptions, and it was argued that "a more constructive long run strategy for business is to reduce unnecessary friction between the sectors and initiate joint efforts whenever common problems can be identified" (p. 57).

But, to return more directly to the specifics of private sector managers' view of BGR, a recent survey reviewing the attitudes of "baby-boom" executives (those under 40 years of age) that was reported in *Fortune* is instructive. This survey, conducted by Rothman and Lichter, found that

> on economic issues, younger managers have come to adopt many beliefs held by their superiors and older colleagues.... Most executives under 40, like those over 40, feel that less government regulation of business is good for the country ... [and] that the federal government ought to be cut back radically. They believe

government is by definition inefficient and are intrigued by the idea of turning over more government services to the private sector.

   They tend to split with other executives . . . by more consistently supporting free markets and free trade. . . . Many say they are against government subsidies to business, bailouts of troubled companies like Chrysler, and protection against foreign competition. . . . While some young executives have been tempted by the idea of a government industrial policy to smooth transition from an industrial to a high-tech service economy, many are skeptical. (Moore, 1985, pp. 75–77)

Although the attitudes reflected in this study do not appear to be as adversarial or confrontational as the attitudes observed in the 1974 UCLA seminar, there is still a clear dislike of government involvement in business matters and a clear preference of private sector over public sector activities.

   Yet, as Sethi, Namiki, and Swanson (1984) have argued, it is important to keep in mind that the appeal of separating business and government, and thus of business and government serving to check or balance the other's power, may have a cyclical basis to it. Sethi et al. argued that the late 1970s' and early 1980s' calls for increased cooperation between business and government were grounded in the slowdown of economic activity and the intensification of foreign competition. They argue that "once the economy picks up, there will be an increase in the desire to maintain a gap between business and government" (p. 247). The implicit proposition in their argument is that good economic times lead to calls for separation, whereas bad economic times lead to calls for cooperation between business and government.

   Along a similar line, a study by Dowling and Schaeffer (1982) shows that antagonism between business and government, as reflected in the editorial content of the *Wall Street Journal*, *Business Week*, and *Fortune*, decreased dramatically from the 1948–1950 period to the 1970–1972 period. According to this study,

   expressed hostility towards government planning and control, opposition to government interference in business, doubt about Keynesian economics, opposition to government expenditures, emphasis on small government, the fear of big government, and hostility to socialism all decreased significantly [from the first period to the second]. On the other hand, acceptance of government planning, regulation, and expenditure on social programs, the evaluation of government in terms of efficiency and effectiveness, and an emphasis on cooperation between business and government increased significantly over the same period [late 1940s versus early 1970]. (Dowling and Schaeffer, 1982, p. 687)

These results show some of the apparent long-term dynamics of private sector attitudes toward government. Change occurs not just with the current issues of the times, but also with long-standing principles of business-government relations such as acceptance of government planning, the needed level of cooperation between business and government, and the evaluation of government efficiency and effectiveness.

In the aggregate, these earlier studies are enlightening in terms of the general tenor and a few details of private sector managers' views of business-government relations. Yet the specifics are still not adequately developed. The motivation for the analysis reported in this chapter was to identify specific attitudes in the private sector managers' views of business-government relations.

Such studies as those cited above are enlightening in terms of the general tenor of private sector managers' attitudes about American business-government relations. Yet, when considering the current conditions of American business-government relations, one wonders what a more narrowly defined set of private sector managers believe. Specifically, what does a group of private sector managers who have been more directly involved with public sector management processes believe about the government as an adversary, about the efficiency and effectiveness of government, and about the appropriate American business-government relationship? In the review of the literature it was found that no study had focused on such a group of "informed" private sector managers.

Cooperative business-government programs have been increasing in numbers during the past decade (McFarland, 1982). One assumption used here was that private sector managers who had participated in such programs would have the experience to form more "informed" attitudes about American business-government relations. These managers should have insights that the more general population of private sector managers do not have. They should be less subject to the negative stereotyping of the public sector that some studies have found (e.g., Driscoll, Cowger, and Egan, 1979). In sum, private sector managers who have participated in a cooperative program should be a more knowledgeable, and therefore a more *informed*, group to survey about business-government relations.

The idea of many cooperative programs is to bring private sector managers into governmental structures in order to assist public sector managers in improving government operations. Cooperative programs should reduce stereotyping by minimizing clear membership in different groups, providing common objectives, and increasing the contact between the groups. Private sector managers who have participated in such programs would therefore be more likely to form their perceptions and attitudes about business-government relations on the basis of experience and not on the "group think" of stereotyping.

To address this concern, an appropriate sample of private sector managers had to be identified. In order to label the sample as "informed private sector managers," we needed to identify a group that had had significant experience-based involvement in public sector management. Our first thought was to identify managers who had held positions in both the public and the private sectors. This approach was rejected, however, because there was no systematic way of determining such a group. A second approach, and the approach selected for this study, was to gain access to a group of private sector managers who had participated in a cooperative business-government program.

THE METHOD

In this study we elicited attitudes about business-government relations from the private sector managers who had participated in the cooperative business-government program Governor's Management Improvement Program (GMIP) for the state of New Jersey (see Chapter 1). Because of their involvement in this program, this set of private sector managers was selected as an appropriate population for looking at the current attitudes toward the state of American business-government relations. Without doubt, this group is still influenced by many positive or negative biases that they took into the cooperative program. Yet, more so than the general population of business executives, they have seen how the public sector works—they have observed firsthand its goals and objectives, its processes, and its restraints.

In the spring of 1985 an attitude survey was mailed to each of the 168 participants in the GMIP. The instrument consisted of 81 questions organized around the following seven general concerns:

1. What is and what ought to be the relationship between business and society?

2. What is and what ought to be the relationship between government and society?

3. What are the appropriate ideals and principles of business-government relations in the United States, and what actually exists in the American business-government relationship?

4. What are the bases for government regulation of business, and how is business participating in the regulatory process?

5. Is industrial policy (used here in the broad sense of the term) appropriate for the United States?

6. How do government managers compare with business managers?

7. What are the appropriate principles and techniques for business-government cooperation?

(The Appendix includes the complete questionnaire.)

The instrument was pretested using MBA students to complete the attitude survey by identifying particularly troublesome items. Respondents in both the pretest and the application were asked to respond to each of the 81 questions by using a 5-point Likert scale (1 = strongly disagree to 5 = strongly agree). Many of the questions in the survey instrument came from or were similar to existing studies of private sector managers' attitudes (Sturdivant and Gintner, 1977; Driscoll et al., 1979; Aupperle, Hatfield, and Carroll, 1983). The other questions were considered exploratory probes for highlighting concerns not clearly addressed in the existing literature on business-government relations.

A more revealing methodology would have been a pretest, post-test design in which changes in responses to the specific questions would be measured before and after involvement in the cooperative program. However, this was not possible because there was no access to the private sector participants until after the program was completed. The survey therefore tapped only postprogram attitudes, and the results are useful primarily as insights into what a more informed group of private sector managers believes about the current state of American business-government relations.*

Study Approach and Design

Figure 3–1 outlines the two basic analyses presented in this chapter. Phase 1 examines the relationships between the resource dependence variable and the measures of potential or actual strategies to deal with BGR. Phase 2 of the study focuses on predictors or antecedents of attitudes toward BGR. Phases 1 and 2 are performed separately and use different statistical methods. Further, different research questions and propositions are addressed in each of the two phases of the analyses outlined in Figure 3–1.

RESEARCH QUESTIONS AND TESTABLE PROPOSITIONS

The Phase 1 research questions are as follows:

(RQI): Are resource dependence and interorganizational strategy (business-government relations) variables related? (Van de Ven and Walker, 1984; Provan et al., 1980; Thompson and McEwen, 1958; Pfeffer and Salancik, 1978).

(RQII): What structure exists in the correlations to explain and better understand relationships between BGR, resource dependence, and interorganizational strategies? (Pfeffer and Salancik, 1978; Van de Ven and Walker, 1984; Steiner and Steiner, 1985).

The following research question and propositions are tested

---

*For a review of the private sector managers' responses on a question-by-question basis, see S. L. Wartick, J. W. Bagby, J. M. Stevens, "Business-Government Relations: Attitudes of Informed Private Sector Managers," *Mid American Journal of Business*, 2 (September 1987): 45–52.

Figure 3–1
Research Design for Study of Resource Dependence, Managerial Experience and Attitudes as Antecedents or Correlates of Business-Government Relations Strategies

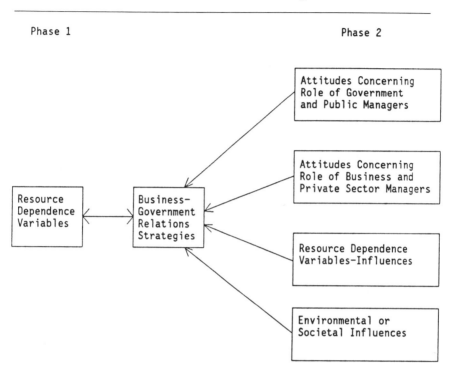

Phase 1   Phase 2

in Phase 2 of the analyses: (RQIII): Do antecedent experiences, attitudes on government, business, resources, and society influence private sector managerial BGR attitudes? The relevant propositions are (a) managerial attitudes concerning government will be associated with BGR strategies, (b) perceptions of the role of business and business managers will be related to BGR strategies, and (c) resource dependence and attitudes on society will be associated with BGR strategies. This question and the three propositions for Phase 2 were developed to be representative of realistic private sector managerial expectations and attitudes that are related to extensive experience-based attitudes of private sector executives.

RESEARCH METHODOLOGY AND PROCEDURES

To examine the research questions and propositions, the resource-based variables to be examined include those with explicit linkages to issues confronting experienced informed
managers who have had intensive experience in industry overall
and in this recent business and government joint project. The
interorganizational strategy (BGR) variables include contemporary, potential, and actual strategies that have been or could be
used by business managers to deal with government, society, or
interest groups. The overall categories and specific variables for
resource and interorganizational relations were not designed to
be exhaustive, but rather relevant, representative dimensions of
realistic BGR attitudes and alternatives.

To examine the research question and propositions related to
the antecedents of business and government relations strategies,
the relationships between government, business, environmental,
and resource-based predictor variables and selected dependent
strategy variables will be examined. The predictor variables include those with explicit linkages to issues confronting informed
managers who have had intensive experience in BGR. The dependent strategy variables include attitudes toward potential and
actual strategies that have been or could be used by business
managers to deal with government or society. The overall categories of antecedent and strategy variables are not designed to
be exhaustive, but rather representative of realistic field-based
executive attitudes.

This study goes beyond past studies by using as respondents
only those top-, mid-, and operational-level private sector managers who have had experience in specific joint partnership
programs, as mentioned previously. Prescribed theoretical, meth-
odological, empirical models or studies in business and government relations are limited. To operationalize the resource and
interorganizational strategy variables, the executives were asked
a series of questions concerning roles of business and government, business-government relations, government effectiveness,
private sector efficiency and effectiveness, regulations, government policy and ways to improve business-government relations,
using a 5-point Likert scale (1 = strongly disagree to 5 = strongly

agree). The resource and interorganizational strategy questions were embedded within these general categories of responses so as not to identify concepts or create response sets. Zero-order correlations were used to investigate interrelationships between the operational measures shown in Figure 3–1.

The research question and propositions in Phase 2 can be appropriately tested using multivariate procedures that permit analyses of relationships between multiple independent or predictor variables and a single dependent variable. Multiple-regression analyses were used to examine the level of statistical association between the government, business, societal, and BGR strategies variables. The use of eight multiple-regression equations for the dependent variables (eight BGR strategies) permitted an assessment of the overall explanatory power of the regression equations and the relative contribution of the independent variables. The use of multiple-regression techniques to answer research question 3 and test the propositions is appropriate because of the study objectives.

The overall resource dependence dimension is operationalized by ten variables that were included in the research design because they represent relevant combined BGR foci and resource dependence issues. There are 20 BGR strategy variables (e.g., cooperative passive, active, co-optative, joint-negotiative, competitive, and conflict) that were used to represent current approaches to different levels of organizational interaction in BGR. This factor was used to determine whether a unified resource dependence diversion existed, and zero-order correlations were used to examine the associations between the resource dependence and BGR measures.

RESULTS

Resource Dependence and Findings

In the interest of parsimony, a factor analysis was first used to reduce the number of variables; however, the varimax rotation of the resource variables produced two dimensions whose reliability indicated that they may be unstable measures. (The results of the factor and related reliability analyses are included in Table

3–1.) Based on the weak results of the reliability test, the complete ten resource dependence variables were used in the analysis.

Table 3–2 presents the zero-order correlations for the 10 resource dependence (RD) and 20 BGR strategy measures represented in the research design in Figure 3–1. The overall pattern of associations is mixed, but certain noteworthy consistencies in the statistically significant correlations do emerge. For example, using $p \geq .10$ as the cutoff and nine or more strong associations, six of the resource dependence (RD) measures exhibit relationships with eight categories of interorganizational relations (IORS/BGR) strategies that have five or more strong associations. The attitude that government depends on business for many of its resources is positively related to the perception that business managers should consult with government managers to improve government, integrate the public responsibility function into strategic management, be proactive in helping government with public needs, actively promote positive BGRs and accept the responsibility to spread the word to the business community when positive BGRs have been experienced. The first BGR posture is more or less passive (i.e., government managers approach business managers for help), but the four other BGRs are more active. This resource variable is also related positively to an active cooperation strategy (i.e., have private sector representatives on government rule-making bodies and involve public interest groups in corporate decision making) and one competitive strategy—have business and government both operate in their own self-interest. Also, the perception that government should be actively opposed is negatively related to the government dependence on business for resource measures. The significant and moderate (e.g., business should get politically involved, $p \leq .10$) relationships between the first RD variable and IORS/BGR variables suggest that the business executives recognize the symbiotic nature of the BGR process. But interestingly, the executives are only somewhat active in following up on this symbiosis.

The second RD variable, societal demands on business deplete critical resources, exhibits two highly and three moderately negative correlations. They suggest that the perceived nature or extent of societal demands may conflict with the desire of business to improve society and/or integrate the public responsibility into

Table 3–1

Factor Analysis Results for Resource Dependence Variables (Varimax Rotation)*

		I**	II**
1.	Government Depends on Business for Resources	.39	-.02
2.	Societal Demands Deplete Private Resources	.13	.19
3.	Government Reduces Resources Required for Economic Development	.01	.56
4.	Policies Create Competitive Advantage for Some Businesses	.64	-.16
5.	Government Managers Use Resources Efficiently	.11	-.53
6.	Government Intervention Decreases Business Efficiency in Resource Use	.05	.59
7.	Business Should Provide Resources to Society	.11	-.10
8.	Government Policies Should Require Joint B–G Funding	.06	-.01
9.	Private Cooperation Determines Effective Resource Use	.50	.01
10.	Policies Should Reflect Scarcity of Resources	.56	.14
Eigenvalue		1.27	1.13
Variance Accounted for		33.6	30.1

---

*A second factor analysis for the IORS variable was not attempted because the relationship of number of cases to variables did not represent an acceptable ratio.

**Cronbach's Alpha Reliability: (A factor loading of .4 was used to create two scales).

      Scale I: .54 (four items)
      Scale II: .34 (three items)

Table 3–2
Zero-Order Correlations Between Resource Use or Effectiveness and Approaches to Business-Government Relations

Resource Use and Effectiveness Variables	APPROACHES TO BUSINESS-GOVERNMENT RELATIONS (BGR) VARIABLES								
	Cooperative								
	Passive			Active					
	Business Managers Should be Receptive to Consulting With Government Managers Who Need Help	BGR Do Not Need Conscious Direction and Should be Allowed to Evolve on Their Own	Business Managers Should Follow the Spirit and Intent of Public Policies	Businesses Should Regulate Themselves to Make Government Regulation Less Likely	Businesses Should Realize That Improving Society is in Their Own Self Interest	Corporations Should Integrate Social Responsibility into Strategic Management	Corporations with Own Standards are Less Likely to be Regulated	Corporations Would Benefit by Helping Government With Community Problems	Business Executives With Positive Government Experiences Should Spread the Word
Government Depends on Business for Many of its Resources	.49[a]	.03	.0	.03	.02	.19[c]	.02	.37[a]	.35[a]
Society Makes Too Many Demands on the Private Sector Which Depletes Critical Resources	−.12	.26[b]	.13	−.21[c]	−.43[a]	−.33[a]	−.12	−.09	−.19[c]
Society Demands Too Much from Government, Reducing Resources for Economic Development	.02	−.17[o]	.22[c]	−.29[b]	−.25[c]	−.12	.09	−.08	−.02
Government Policies Can Make Some Business More Profitable by Creating Competitive Advantage	.18[o]	.08	.0	.11	.02	−.05	.02	.22[c]	.07
Government Managers are Efficient in Using Resources	.12	.11	.10	.06	.33[a]	.27[b]	.29[b]	.19	.07
Regardless of Intent, Government Intervention Decreases Business Resource Efficiency	−.02	.07	−.11	−.17[d]	−.15[d]	−.06	−.09	−.08	.01
Corporations Should Provide Resources for Achieving Societal Objectives	.19[c]	−.23[c]	.13	.13	.69[a]	.62[b]	.27	.11	.32[b]
Public Policies that Affect Business Should Require Joint Funding	−.05	−.22[c]	.07	.02	.11	.26[b]	.16[d]	.14	.15[d]
Effective Government Resource Use Depends on Private Sector Cooperation	.16[o]	−.05	.01	.19[c]	.16[d]	.05	.19[c]	.17[d]	.34[a]
Government Policies Must Reflect How Scarce Resources are Becoming	.04	−.02	−.16[d]	.10	.07	.23[c]	.04	.05	.19[c]

[a]$p \leq .001$; [b]$p \leq .01$; [c]$p \leq .05$; [d]$p \leq .10$

Table 3–2 (continued)

APPROACHES TO BUSINESS-GOVERNMENT RELATIONS (BGR) VARIABLES										
Cooperative		Cooptative				Negotiative Joint		Competitive		Conflict
Active										
Cooperative BGR have to be Followed up for a Time to be Effective	Private Sector Managers are More Responsive than Government Managers	Businesses Affected by Regulation Should Help Government in Formulation of Policy	Government Decision Making Bodies Should Include Business Representatives	Government Representatives Should be on Business Boards of Directors	Interest Groups Other Than Business Should be Involved in Developing Public Policies that Affect Business	Government Regulations Should Require Cooperative BGR	B-G Conflicts Should be Resolved by Neutral Third Party Negotiators	To Protect Business, Managers Should Become More Involved in Politics	Business and Government Managers Should Operate in Their Own Self Interest	Business Should Actively Oppose Government if Profits are Affected
−.06	.02	.25[c]	.25[c]	.02	.21[c]	.05	.09	.18[d]	.25[c]	−.23[c]
−.05	−.06	−.21[c]	.19[c]	.02	−.13	.30[b]	.07	.01	.09	.15[d]
.16[d]	−.05	−.13	.10	.02	−.23[c]	.03	.03	−.01	−.06	.19[c]
.23[c]	.05	.07	.10	−.06	.05	.06	.0	.12	.19[c]	.11
−.20[c]	.19[c]	.25[c]	.07	.18[d]	.18[d]	.15[d]	.08	.02	.16[d]	−.23[c]
.0	−.39[a]	.0	.04	−.31[b]	.08	.07	.0	.23[c]	−.16[d]	.21[c]
.19[c]	.15[d]	.35[a]	.07	.31[b]	.04	.14	.15[d]	.15[d]	−.06	.01
.13	.22	.16	.17[d]	.35[a]	−.23[c]	.31[b]	.39[a]	.15	−.06	.18[d]
.19[c]	−.01	.31[b]	.09	−.08	.06	.36[a]	.05	.27[b]	.03	.06
.27[b]	.05	.08	.09	.08	−.17[d]	.33[a]	.22[c]	.14	.02	.07

[a] $p \leq .001$; [b] $p \leq .01$; [c] $p \leq .05$; [d] $p \leq .10$

51

strategic management. The moderately negative findings for business regulating itself, spreading positive information, and proactively helping government highlight the negative impact of societal demands on business. This is an important set of results because the cooperative posture toward government found earlier does not apply to *society* overall. Even the positive correlations take more of a passive (i.e., let BGR evolve on their own without conscious direction), negotiative (legislate cooperation), or even a conflictual approach to government. These findings suggest that a complex business-government society dynamic is in operation (i.e., societal pressures exist for both business and government).

Another resource variable relationship suggests that societal demands may promote disequilibrium in BGR because the pressures may be too diffuse until government translates them into specific policies. The next resource-based variable, government creating competitive advantages for certain industries or businesses, only moderately affects the IORS/BGR of actively promoting BGR, following up on cooperative efforts, and business and government operating in their own self-interest. The perception of how efficiently government managers use resources is positively related to the IORS/BGR variables of improving society in self-interest, establishing own standards, integrating public responsibility into management, proactively helping government, actively promoting BGR, and perceiving the private sector as being more responsive. The negative association with following up on cooperative efforts supports the attitude that government intervention may not be the most efficient way to deal with societal problems. This, of course, leaves open the questions of cause and effect of societal problems and who should resolve them.

There are two strong and two moderate associations between the government intervention–decreasing business efficiency, resource variables and the interorganizational variables. The strongest relationships are negative, which implies that the private sector executives do not perceive the value of government representation in private sector decision making or other interventions. The two moderate positive relationships suggest that resource use may be a significant consideration in how these executives view relations with government.

Resource variable seven, business providing resources for society, exhibits several powerful associations that suggest that a proactive, strategic use of resources to improve society is in the best self-interest of business. The moderately strong correlations relating to government representatives, standards, and consultation capture an overall positive, proactive attitude toward active cooperation or co-optation of government.

A more specific resource variable, requiring public policies to specify joint business-government funding, has several strong and moderate associations with co-optative, negotiative, and active cooperation variables. The strongest relationships are with the co-optative-negotiative strategies, such as involving government representatives in private sector decisions, using third party negotiations in disputes, and having government regulations require cooperation of business and government. Other moderate relationships are with private sector being more responsive and not just letting BGRs evolve on their own. These results suggest a need for joint negotiation and mutual co-optative BGR strategies, but at "arms length."

The strongest associations of the private sector cooperation with government variables show that the executives recognize resource usage as a two-way street, with government effectiveness at least partially being determined by private sector cooperation. The strongest correlations show that government regulations, cooperation, spreading positive information, business being proactive in helping government, possibly getting involved politically, following up on cooperative efforts, establishing own standards, and self-regulation are potential strategies to use in operationalizing the mutual resource interdependence between business and government.

The associations for the last resource variable, making government policies reflect resource scarcity, appear to represent a need for negotiated and joint cooperative strategies, including integrating the public responsibility function into business strategy. The results of the preceding analysis are discussed in more detail in a subsequent section; however, resource scarcity appears to represent a basis for negotiated and joint cooperative strategies. The overall pattern of correlations suggests that a complex, apparently mutual exclusive set of perceptions exists simultaneously for these executives. This seeming paradox and its

relevance for further theory development and managerial practice is discussed further.

Dominant BGR Variables

The preceding results focused on the relationships between
the 10 resource-related and 20 IORS variables; however, another
interesting focus is that of dominant IORS. As implied in the
previous analyses, some conflict existed, but certain cooperative,
co-optative, and negotiative-joint IORS were prevalent (five or
more strong correlations). The most common IORS were (a) integrating the public responsibility function into corporate strategic management; (b) opposing government if profits were
affected; (c) proactively helping government with problems; (d)
improving society in self-interest; (e) spreading positive information; (f) having government regulations require cooperation;
(g) involving interest groups in decision making; and (h) actively
promoting business-government relations. Other IORS variables
with several statistically significant associations across the resource variables were business establishing own standards; private sector being more responsive; government representatives
on private decision-making bodies; letting BGRs evolve on their
own, and involving interest groups in corporate decision making.
The primary IORS represented are cooperative-co-optative, with
one clear conflict strategy. The overall tenor of the strategies
appears to represent a passive-cooperative/co-optative to mild
conflict continuum. The primarily cooperative attitudes have
some inherent complexities in terms of their implications for
practice, especially the perceptions that go beyond the "arms-
length" or "battling business" model used by at least one current
advocate of improving government efficiency (e.g., see Goodsell,
1984).

Informed Managerial Attitudes and BGR Strategies

Table 3–3 includes the summary regression results that analyze
the associations between the predictor and BGR strategy–approach variables. The overall pattern of the multiple-regression

Table 3–3
Summary of Regression Results for Managerial Attitudes on Business-Government Relations Strategies[a,b]

Business-Government Relations Strategies-Approaches	ANTECEDENT MANAGERIAL ATTITUDES AND FOCI											
	Attitudes Concerning Role of Government and Public Managers							Attitudes Concerning Business and Private Sector Managers				
	Aging Industries Need Govt. Support	Govt. Has Centralized Decisionmaking	Govt. Can Determine Which Industries to Support	Only Govt. Can Deal With High Unemployment	Criticism Undermines Govt. Effectiveness	Govt. Managers are Impartial in Applying Policies	Govt. Managers are as Professional as Business Managers	If Business Regulated Itself, Then No Govt. Interference	American Management Systems are Outdated	Business Managers Talk to Executive Branch of Government	Business Managers Consider Public Interest in Decisions	Business Managers Should Get Involved in Politics
Corporations Should Provide Resources for Societal Objectives	.21			−.22		.25	.15					
Corporations Should Integrate Social Responsibility With Strategic Management			−.24								.34	.29
Corporations with Internal Standards are Less Likely to be Regulated								.18			.21	
Business and Govt. Managers Treat Each Other as Adversaries					.17							.43
Govt. Should Require Business to Develop Cooperative Approaches		.34							−.34			
Business Managers Should Realize that Improving Social and Economic Conditions is in Self Interest		.24										
Business-Govt. Relations Should be Allowed to Evolve on Their Own	−.16		−.22		−.25							
Business Managers Should Spread the Word When They Have Positive Relations with Govt.		.21	.13			.16	.13				.30	

a* = p ≤ .05; ** = p ≤ .01; *** = p ≤ .001
b Standardized coefficients are used to identify the relative contribution of each variable.

Table 3–3 (continued)

ANTECEDENT MANAGERIAL ATTITUDES AND FOCI													
Attitudes Concerning Business and Private Sector Managers					Resource Dependence Variables				Political, Environmental and Societal Influences				Summary Statistics
Business and Govt. Should Operate in Self-Interest	Business Decisionmaking is More Effective Than Government	Business Managers Face Risks in Voluntary Contributions	Business Managers Talk With Legislative Branch of Government	Business Managers not Accountable to Society	Public Policies Should Reflect Scarce Resources	Too Many Demands on Private Sector Depletes Resources	Govt. Managers are Efficient in Using Resources	Govt. Depends on Business for Most Resources	Govt. Is Responsible for Social Equity	Politicans are Always Running for Office	Fiscal Uncertainty Promotes Business-Govt. Cooperation	Free Market is Best for National Economic Development	R^2 F-Value
						−.21			−.33				.46 9.93***
					15	−.21			−.17				.53 12.95***
−.19	.18						.24					.17	.33 5.00***
			.18						.23	.31	14		.43 8.57***
					−.32	−.16					.35	.16	.55 14.1***
		−.19				−.30	.18		−.31				.49 11.26***
			.−21			.20		.38*	.24				.38 6.93***
													.38 8.53***

a* = p ≤ .05; ** = p ≤ .01; *** = p ≤ .001
bStandardized coefficients are used to identify the relative contribution of each variable.

results captured by the summary statistics (R^2; F-value) at the bottom of Table 3–3 is consistent and valuable because it provides an answer for the research question. Each of the eight regression equations is statistically significant and accounts for a low of 33 percent variation explained (for the internal standards strategy) to a high of 55 percent for the government requiring a cooperative strategy. These statistically significant levels of variation explained suggest that the predictor variables are important correlates of the dependent BGR variables. Based on these results, the research question can be answered in the affirmative (i.e., certain of the managerial attitudes measured here are important predictors of managerial BGR approaches). The implications of these relationships are presented and discussed in more detail subsequent to the analysis of the results relating to the propositions.

To obtain further information regarding tests for the propositions, the individual BGR strategy and related set or spread of predictors have to be examined separately. Each BGR strategy is unique in substance, and the distribution of predictor variables and their relative strength are assessed by the standardized value in the table. Each block of independent variables in Figure 3–1 is represented by separate categories from top to bottom at the left in Table 3–3.

The first BGR strategy, corporations should provide resources for achieving societal objectives, is interesting in that 46 percent of the variation is explained and four of the six antecedents are related to government or public managers. For example, if government managers were thought to be impartial in the application of public policies, these business managers would be positively predisposed to providing corporate resources. Two other positive predictors were centralized government decision making and perceptions of public managers as being equally professional to business managers. Together, these positive predictors indicate that professional, impartial, and centralized (presumably less particularistic) public management would induce more favorable corporate responses to contributing resources for societal needs.

The negative antecedents of corporate responses are also enlightening because they indicate potentially conflicting social attitudes. The strongest negative predictor, government is responsible for social equity, and the other two (only government can deal with high unemployment; too many societal demands deplete resources) leave open the question of who these managers think should perform the societal functions. The associations also highlight the issue of thresholds (i.e., an effective government would elicit corporate resources, but how much is too much).

The second BGR strategy, corporations should integrate the social responsibility function into strategic management, has over half the variance accounted for, with six antecedents. Two of the strongest variables are business-related predictors, business managers should consider the public interest in their decision making and get involved in politics. They suggest an activist and socially responsible posture for the managers, whereas the two resource dependence variables recognize the negative effect of too many public policies on scarce corporate resources. The negative influences of government's sole responsibility for equity and dealing with unemployment are also observed, and bring into question the relative efficacy of public versus private responses to societal problems.

The third proactive BGR strategy, corporations with internal BGR and social responsibility standards are less likely to be regulated, exhibits a pattern different from the first two. Less variation is accounted for overall (33 percent). A resource dependence variable is the strongest predictor of this strategy, and the role of business/private sector managers in self-regulation is the chief predictor. These relationships may be interpreted to mean that if government managers are perceived as efficient in the use of resources, private sector managers are more likely to develop internal BGR strategies and public interest standards. These associations may reflect critical resource issues that highlight the interdependence of public and private managers and their mutual focus on joint partnerships. This is especially salient in light of the positive influence of the free market variable. The negative influence of the "operating in self-interest" variable would seem to indicate that there is explicit recognition that the private and public sectors cannot afford conflict or explicitly compete with each other.

The fourth strategy of business and public managers, treating each other as adversaries, had 43 percent of the variation explained primarily by political, environmental/societal, and business role variables, with one government role influence. The strong influence of the "political" variables on this strategy is noteworthy. Business managers getting involved in politics was the strongest predictor, and politicians always running for office was the second strongest predictor. Other interesting predictors were that government is perceived to be responsible for social equity, and business managers are not accountable to society. Taken together, these results for the adversarial strategy appear to be more strongly influenced by the instability rather than the centrality of the political process for resolving the ambiguity of social equity and accountability responsibilities inherent in the public sector.

The fifth dependent variable, government requiring business to develop cooperative approaches with public managers, had the most variation explained (55 percent), with rather interesting findings. Strong positive predictors were fiscal uncertainty, the ability of government to determine which industries to support, and the view that public policies should reflect scarce societal resources. Also noteworthy was the strong negative effect of the view that American management systems are outdated and the positive influence of the free market on national economic development. These relationships reflect a bifurcated perspective on business-government interaction, given the juxtaposition of the belief in free markets, outdated American management systems, and the governmental ability to determine an industrial policy (either implicit or explicit). Further, there appears to be an implicit recognition in the results of the opposing duality inherent in dealing with fiscal uncertainty (along with scarce resources) and the value of mandatory cooperation between business and government.

Business managers recognizing that improvement of the social-economic environment is in their self-interest is the sixth approach to BGR. Three major negative influences were government being responsible for social equity, too many societal demands depleting business resources, and private sector risk taking involuntary or philanthropic contributions. These predictors are very salient to the BGR strategy issue that centers around the sufficiency criterion (i.e., how much is enough?). What is the threshold at which societal demands on the private sector become destructive? Will voluntary contributions be riskier than government requiring compliance? In the area of social needs where criteria are ill defined, there is a legitimate question of how boundaries can be determined. The finite resource pool may require careful mediation in the resource allocation processes.

The next variable, BGRs evolving on their own, captures the traditional laissez faire model. This interpretation is supported by the predictors. For example, the positive influence of the belief that government is dependent on business for resources, the negative influences or criticism undermining government effectiveness, government being able to determine industrial support, aging industrial needing public support, and government being responsible for social equity imply that government has a social (not controlling) role where industrial-economic judgments have to be made. The influence of many societal demands and the negative influence of discussions with legislators support this interpretation. These associations add further evidence to the idea that a major efficiency-equity dilemma exists for private sector managers in determining corporate BGR strategies.

The last BGR strategy examined here, private sector managers spreading the word about positive interactions with government, exhibits strong associations with attitudes concerning government. For instance, government having centralized decision making, determining industrial support, public managers being impartial and professional are positive influences on spreading the word. Also, business managers contacting the executive branch of government (agencies, elected and nonelected officials) has a positive effect on spreading information. These findings for the last variable suggest that if government decision makers are impartial, professional, and cooperative, positive associations will develop and be promoted by these corporate managers.

SUMMARY AND DISCUSSION FOR PHASE 1

The results for both the practical and the theoretical dimensions of business and government relations indicate that extensive interdependence is perceived, but that private sector managerial actions to operationalize this state of affairs are unclear. The multibillion-dollar government purchases of goods, services, information, and support from the private sector, gov-

ernment regulation of business, effects of national taxation, demands for trade restrictions, monetary and fiscal policies,
national deficits and the reliance of government on business for
revenue highlight the mutual dependence between government
and business. However, regulation, trade imbalances, the Grace
Commission, tax reform, so-called corporate bailouts, international pressures, industrial policy issues, defense industry indictments, and, not least of all, incomplete theory to explain
these relationships argue for more mutual understanding.

This exploratory study has presented certain patterns and findings that help in understanding BGR in terms of resource dependence and interorganizational concepts, but the results also
suggest that further development is needed. The findings illustrate that positive BGRs (i.e., cooperation, negotiation, joint processes) are intellectually desirable, but on a practical level they
are not strategically or operationally implemented. The symbiotic relationships and resource interdependence between corporate and public IORS appear to be accepted cognitively, but
not behaviorally.

Another phenomenon observed here that is related to BGR may
be called a "threshold effect." That is, positive business, society,
and government relations are viewed as necessary, but too many
societal demands may saturate joint private and public managerial decision-making processes. It appears that negative reactions from business increase when the tempo of demands from
government and society increases. This is an important strategic
issue because this conflict arises at precisely the critical time
when more cooperative processes are needed. More or less trivial
joint programs or partnerships may be designed incrementally
to deal with routine problems, but the major test is with more
critical occurrences (e.g., the Tylenol scares, Bhopal Indian-In-
stitute, West Virginia chemical leaks, Three Mile Island, corporate indictments, government bailouts, etc.), which require more
in-depth strategic attention to BGR.

Overall, the correlation findings show that the directions and
levels of interdependence among business, government, and society are understood superficially but are not clear in terms of a
cause-effect or initiator-reactor cycle. For instance, does government moderate the relationship between business and society,
or does business "cause" (by inaction or action) government to

act in the best interests of society when problems associated with the public safety or public interest occur? Should business operate in its own self-interest by proactively managing its external BGR and IORS to preclude or prevent problems? The origins of problems in the cycle of causes and effects are historical, complex, and difficult to determine; however, the interdependence among business actions, government intervention, and societal demands requires further strategic and contingency analysis that better defines strategic priorities for corporations.

One complex issue highlighted by the findings is the perceived role of government. For these executives, government generally was not perceived as responsive or efficient in resource use. The strategic lesson for business is to determine what activates that apparently nonresponsive and inefficient mechanism. Is it spontaneous, reactive, or random? If government intervention is required by society or inherent constitutional objectives, unresponsive, and inefficient (which is not being examined here), then what strategies must be developed by business? Actively opposing government, getting politically involved, and operating in terms of self-interest were alternative strategies that exhibited some relationships with resource dependence perceptions, but were not pervasive or highly significant. These findings point to the need for a more proactive, anticipatory strategic posture for business to balance priorities in business-government relations.

One dilemma represented in the correlation findings is that the need for cooperative, co-optative, and/or joint-negotiative strategies is perceived, but their economic or operational validity does not appear to have been established. One model, a mutual "keep business (or government) at arms length" approach, does not appear to be inclusive of the complexity and different levels of mutual resource dependence. "Partnership" approaches may presume too little or too much dependence. The economic efficiency of pure cooperation or conflict/competitive models for BGR is not easily demonstrated. Current industrial policy or partnership concepts are subject to volatile interpretations because they do not appear to be sufficiently complete in accounting for mutual resource dependence issues.

The associations answer the first two research questions; however, they also further illustrate the complexity and ambiguity associated with business-government interaction. The findings show that the issue of resource dependence may be a central show that the issue of resource dependence may be a central referent for analyzing BGR strategies. The associations here suggest that one way for business to approach this integration is through appropriate strategic management analyses where the role of BGR is thoroughly forecasted, documented, and prioritized in terms of other competing or generic strategies. These strategic analyses would have to include a valid approach to contingent analysis where if—then logic may have to be designed. For instance, if government is inefficient in using or negatively affects business resources, would competitive or conflict strategies or models be the most effective? If government is needed for support, is the Chrysler-Lockheed approach best? If international competition is perceived as operating unfairly, should government be pressured by business to adopt trade restrictions? The overall resource and operational substance of a given issue or problem should be thoroughly understood in any given if—then circumstance.

The contemporary resource dependence analysis and examples presented here can only be considered a starting point for further analysis because the current BGR topic does not appear to have a well-codified, theoretical, or cumulative empirical foundation. Can, or should, business and government cooperate to create regulations? Should private sector representatives sit on government decision-making bodies, and is the converse appropriate? What is the value of the co-participation/co-determination model used in other parts of the world? What steps can be taken by business to address the longer-term resource dependence, substantive and strategic interdependence with government issues? One clear answer found in the results appears to be that the current unidimensional arms-length, bureaucracy-bashing, hat-in-hand, or partnership approaches are inadequate as business strategies. The correlations illustrate that growing complexity of business and government interdependence is not well understood, analyzed, or effective but could be if valid conceptual frameworks are established and tested systematically, using practical contexts.

Predictors of BGR Summary

Most of the summary results of the regression analyses in phase 2 of the study were statistically significant, interesting in terms of explanation, heartening in terms of research directions, and supportive of the research question and propositions. They also may have serious implications and present dilemmas for students of business-government relations and corporate strategies.

The findings clearly suggest that the attitudes of experienced private sector executives are related to the business-government relations variables examined here. The perceived roles of business, effectiveness of business, resource dependence, impartiality-professionalism, and effectiveness of public managers are also statistically significant antecedents of BGRs. For example, if public managers are perceived as being impartial, professional, efficient in their use of resources and cognizant of the government's dependence on business for resources, then these private sector managers would be supportive of providing corporate resources for societal objectives, integrating social responsibility functions into strategic management, and developing internal BGR standards. However, with several influences, such as politicians always running for office, government being, and business managers not being accountable for social programs, and too many societal demands on business, business managers see the value of being politically active (and/or taking more laissez-faire approaches to social responsiveness).

These results tend to support the view that there are multiple, probably opposing forces working for and against positive or cooperative BGRs. The results also suggest that this dualism is influenced by internally inconsistent perceptions. The effects of high unemployment and fiscal uncertainty associated with international competition and the efficacy of American management systems illustrate that few linear assumptions can be made. Is government the primary mediator of external or global economic forces and mechanisms, such as import quotas, tariffs, or industrial policies? Or, is this globalization of economies just a natural widening of the free "marketplace" for business in which government support is not needed?

Should adversarial models be used to structure BGR strategies? The results here indicate that this kind of approach activates "political" strategies and defines government as being responsible for social-equity programs. Other findings suggest that cooperative BGRs are positively influenced by the attitude that government has the ability to determine industrial policy, but in contradiction to that, public policies should reflect scarce resources. This kind of duality pervades the results and intimates that the boundaries or degrees of interdependence in BGR are not conceptually clear.

In addition, the results here support the correlation findings and show that these business managers appear to implicitly recognize that there can be too many demands on corporations. That is, there is a point at which societal demands may deplete corporate resources. This introduces the related strategy question of the BGR effectiveness if government is responsible and accountable for social programs. The interesting question is, "where do corporate self-interest and accountability begin and end?" If government uses business resources for dealing with social needs, why should corporate managers get involved? The results here demonstrate that government, in the political and uncertainty context, may not be perceived as the most efficient, impartial, or effective arbiter of the social resource allocation processes. This leaves open the question of business responsibility or interdependence with government.

Implications and Continuing Issues

The positive foundation for further research and practice provided by the results is heartening in that it illustrates the complexity of the relationships among experience, attitudes, and BGR strategies. However, several important implications and dilemmas remain. The persistent duality between positive approaches to BGR and the roles of accountability of business managers is perplexing. These managers see the value of explicitly integrating BGR into corporate strategy, but they also perceive government as being responsible and accountable for social programs. A key question is whether government is perceived as being sufficiently effective and impartial to be a mediator of societal demands on business? Is it possible for either business or government to do this? Who is the most efficient resource allocator for social programs? If business is not socially responsible/accountable, must government, which is perceived as being inefficient, force it to be? Direct social attacks on business may not be beneficial for society, business, or government in the long run.

A central implication of the results that deserves more attention is how to design mechanisms to deal with common business-government problems and the corresponding resource allocation processes. There are also serious implications for government managers who are accountable for social programs and also maintain the viability of resource providers such as business. What are the most effective BGR approaches for both private and public managers?

The results here indicate that for these business managers, cooperative BGRs are not necessarily the most economical. Their economic viability to either the public or the private sector has not really been demonstrated possibly because political variables and fiscal uncertainty require specific actions. Should business and government managers be held jointly accountable? Are joint actions required to stabilize international forces beyond the separate sphere of either the private or the public sector?

There may have been value to a mutual arm's length approach to BGR in less turbulent times, but the findings from the analysis in this chapter indicate that there has been sufficient merging of public and private interests to systematically reexamine the value of various BGR models. Some integrated perspectives on responsibility for societal programs are required. Neither business nor government can jointly or separately meet every demand because there may be bottomless pits; therefore, integrative resource allocation responses must be designed. Neither sector should control the other, but system-based mechanisms and strategies have to be designed. The complexity and uncertainty in the current global competition for resources suggest that the researchers and practitioners involved with BGR are facing a challenge that needs to carefully define the parameters of appropriate models.

CONCLUSIONS

The purpose of these correlations and regression studies was to empirically assess whether there were relationships among managerial experience, attitudes, and business-government relations strategies. By using private sector managers experienced in a business-government project focusing on cooperation between private and public sector managers, the results of the regression analyses answered the research questions and supported the propositions. The overall statistically significant relationships demonstrated that managerial attitudes concerning the role of government and public managers, role of business and private managers, perceptions of resource dependence, and certain environmental influences were associated with various business-government relations strategies. The effectiveness, impartiality, and professionalism of public managers and government affected whether the managers should provide corporate resources for societal objectives, integrate social responsibility with strategic management, treat government as an adversary, see social-economic issues as self-interest, or just allow BGRs to evolve on their own.

Attitudes concerning the role of business in society and resource dependence variables influenced whether corporations should develop internal standards, be required to cooperate with government, and/or spread positive information concerning BGR. Environmental issues such as fiscal uncertainty, politicians always running for office, and responsibility for social/equity needs were strongly related to cooperative and adversarial strategies. The results illustrated the usefulness of combining a theoretical BGR perspective with practical antecedents of managerial BGR strategies.

One inescapable conclusion is that these managers exhibited a dual or bifurcated set of attitudes. That is, the effectiveness of current American management systems may not be seen as being capable of dealing with valid, complex environmental changes, but neither was government. However, impartial, professional, and effective government was perceived as being related to the willingness to provide resources for social objectives. The traditional battling-business, arms-length, or extreme "partnership" models by themselves are not entirely appropriate approaches to solving the BGR strategy conundrum. Regardless of efficiency, should government determine who is responsible, and mandate cooperation/regulation? Can voluntary business approaches be counterproductive? The results argue strongly that there is a central role and need for effective "system" resource–allocation processes that have to be designed into business-government relations.

The implications and remaining questions highlight the need for informed practice and further research on the role of government/public managers as mediators of societal needs, the role of business in developing proactive BGR strategies, the issue of effective resource allocation for social responsibility, and how business and government should cooperate. Two major interdependent dilemmas are how private and public managers can design mutual strategies to deal with or even moderate the common political, international, and fiscal resource uncertainty that confronts both sectors.

CHAPTER 4

Informed Public Managerial Perceptions of Business-Government Relations

An analysis of organizations from the perspective of comparative government can place our understanding of organizations in a refreshing perspective. However, in order to understand the day-to-day political dynamics of organization, it is also necessary to explore the detailed processes through which people engage in politics. For this purpose, it is useful to return to Aristotle's idea that politics stems from a diversity of interests, and trace how this diversity gives rise to the "wheeling and dealing," negotiation, and other processes of coalition building and mutual influence that shape so much of organizational life.

An organization's politics is most clearly manifest in the conflicts and power plays that sometimes occur center stage, and in the countless interpersonal intrigues that provide diversions in the flow of organizational activity. More fundamentally, however, politics occurs on an ongoing basis, often in a way that is invisible to all but those directly involved.

GARETH MORGAN
Images of Organization

If there is a major unifying link between the past political-economic context of the United States and the future, it is the domain of business-government interdependence, which many have characterized as politics of the highest order. With the evolution to a global economy and the existing central role of government in dealing with intractable societal and economic problems, the significance of relationships between government and business has become increasingly visible and financially significant. The traditional adversarial posture on either the public or the private side of the BGR fence somehow fails to address the practical and policy needs facing public managers. Though multiple forms of public-private partnerships have been proposed and tried in various settings, there is a lack of consensus on what optimal approaches should be used (Adams, 1983). The purpose of the study reported in this chapter is to identify current issues and possible approaches to the substance of business-government relations (BGR) from the perspective of public managers who have been involved in a joint program with private executives.

RELEVANT CONTEXTUAL ISSUES

Few would state that the relations between governments and businesses are mutually beneficial or effective. In fact, the opposite is suggested if the recent literature and practice can be used as benchmarks. For example, Goodsell (1984) outlined and analyzed the approach used by the Grace Commission to improve government. He concluded that the "whole people" would not be served by this approach, which he characterized as an attack on government. Despite critical reviews in several national and media forums, Peter Grace pressed the very visible attack on "waste" until recently because both societal and governmental entities supported this adversarial approach (Kelman, 1985; Grace, 1985). Demands for deregulation, budget deficits, persistent calls for reduction in the size of government, and negative comments directed toward public servants from political leaders witnessed a frustration with the complex role of government and public managers. In this contemporary climate of mutual suspicion and stereotyping, it is problematic *whether*, not necessarily how, BGR can be made more effective.

Adding to the perplexity of the situation are the recent pronouncements regarding the role of business in BGR. Governmental "bailouts" of auto and aircraft companies, massive chemical leaks, widespread "insider trading" and fraud on Wall Street, check-kiting by financial institutions, fraud in defense procurement industries, and lack of industrial competitiveness worldwide highlight the issue of whether business is itself capable of internal adjustments and systemic adaptation. The paucity of consensual values, declining confidence in political and business leaders, primacy of special interest ideologies, repeated market failures, and hostile attitudes toward elements of the traditional business, government, and social structure indicate that there are more fragmenting than integrating forces at work in the system overall. This milieu of competing influences forms a backdrop for the policy and pragmatic objectives that public managers must achieve in BGR (see, for example, Savas, 1982).

Public Managerial Models and BGR

Confronting the many times intractable problems and dilemmas found in society and business-government relations are several layers of local, regional, state, and federal managers (Ingraham and Ban, 1986). Not only do these levels of government confront numerous, persistent, episodic, and substantively diverse pressures, but they also have multiple constituency and objectives' environments (Ring and Perry, 1985; Stevens and McGowan, 1983). Complementing this diversity of influences is the conceptual ambiguity of the public manager's task (Rainey et al., 1976; Perry and Kraemer, 1983). From the exhortations of Woodrow Wilson in 1887 to the laissez faire model enunciated by President Reagan in 1986 (*Fortune*, 1986), the interim period catalogued or championed such public managerial approaches as principles of public administration, neutral competence, decision making, generic management, administrative science, policy analysis, political science paradigms, and public management (Perry and Kraemer, 1983). However, even the most recent analysis demonstrates the equivocality of the accepted models, especially with reference to interdependence with the private sector (Moore, 1984). This challenge may also apply to the private sector models of management (Geneen, 1984).

Because the public management paradigm is particularly elusive and subject to many interpretations in a demanding, turbulent environment, the role of public managers at all levels of government is continually evolving. The pervasiveness of government-business interdependence in such activities as direct purchases, international trade, regulation, import controls, antitrust actions, securities exchange monitoring, and environmental protection requires systematic guidelines that are not forthcoming from the "bottom-line" private sector, political controllers, or "neutral competence" public sector models.

It has long been recognized that effective public managers are forced to behave differently than private managers because of multiple restraints on their power. The effects are often based on political contexts and demands for accountability. Public sector purposes, organizations, people, managerial motivation, and diverse, ambiguous performance measures certainly complicate the development of generalized public manager models. However, given the number and complexity of the demands for accountability, they are likely to continue rather than abate. With the need to understand the more visible roles of government executives, more inclusive and systematic studies of key public managerial activities and relationships are needed.

One intent of the study presented in this chapter is to further develop the concept of public managers dealing with business by examining and codifying some of the attitudes of informed top-level state executives who have had direct experience in a well-developed cooperative approach with top-level corporate executives. In this way an important component of the public managerial task can be circumscribed more specifically to illuminate critical strategic and power issues that will undoubtedly confront public executives in the future (Murray and Jick, 1981). Many would argue that business and government should be separate and kept that way, but this unidimensional view may not be relevant in a world of competing, global interdependencies in which cooperative or co-determination approaches have proved successful in other diverse developing national economies.

Perspectives on Public Managerial Needs

It has become axiomatic in some circles to state that more cooperation between business and government will result in mutual understanding of each other's problems or demands, and therefore result in improved relations. Though stated frequently and with much fervor, this particular proposition has not been supported in depth or implemented extensively across all levels of government. Further, recent evidence, such as the Grace Commission, bureaucracy-bashing by certain governmental or elected administrators, and lobbying efforts, suggest an evolution toward the opposite (Goodsell, 1984). There are instances of the federal government "bailing out" certain private sector industries or corporations, and there are some examples of successful local partnerships; however, many unanswered questions and key concerns remain (Adams, 1983; Kelman, 1985; Grace, 1985).

Complicating the relationships between business and government have been mutual, strong, persistent, negative stereotypes and "myths" about managers in each sector. Public managers see themselves as routinely putting in long days, being accountable to the people, and being on the "cutting edge" of social policy. Conversely, private sector managers view the public manager as not having to meet a payroll, as not having to show a profit, as retiring on the job, and as facing no demands from consumers (Driscoll et al., 1979). A recent study showed that both public sector and private sector managers grudgingly admitted that some demands are unique to each sector, but that they cling to the idea that "their counterparts have more room for improvement than they do" (Driscoll et al., 1979, p. 54).

The dilemma of mutually negative perceptions between public and private managers clearly exists, but its counterpart—the question of how to achieve effective cooperation, as opposed to competition or the conflict most recently exhibited by the Grace Commission approach—is still largely unresolved. For example, Kelman recently concluded that the government "horror stories" of mismanagement, $91 screws, procurement system problems, seized assets, quality, hospital management, and building maintenance costs are gross exaggerations. Kelman also stated that the Grace Commission was headline-grabbing, and he recommended procedures to solve the apparent problems. Further, Kelman believes that the Grace Commission betrayed the objectives of the war on waste. In his rebuttal, Peter Grace (chairman of the Grace Commission) admitted that certain errors existed in the Commission report, but stated further that "the inescapable fact is that waste and inefficiency do exist in government, and exist on a massive scale" (Grace, 1985; p. 111). Grace did not consider policy to be immune from examination, and concluded that taxpayers resent having their money wasted whether it is a result of "operating inefficiencies or legislative policy" (Grace, 1985; p. 121).

These recent views represent a conflictual and counterproductive approach, which suggests that further improvements in government-business relations may not evolve naturally and are needed as the issues become more central. If sound public-private partnerships, negotiative or joint initiatives are to be developed, they must proceed from a valid foundation of informed knowledge, not from the popular bureaucracy or business-bashing strategies now in fashion. These ever-present dilemmas that concern business-government relations have even more significance, since public management itself is experiencing a self-searching and renewal process (Ingraham and Ban, 1986). In addition, the implications of mutual negative attitudes for various cooperative initiatives get mired down in discussions of costs of regulations, globalization of the worldwide economy, the welfare state, import or trade controls, and, more recently, the role of government in industrial policy (Reich, 1983).

Because many complex issues pertinent to the substance of business-government relations persist, one purpose of this analysis is to examine the attitudes of top-level state managers who have recently participated in a joint cooperative effort to improve public sector management and decision making. This study goes beyond the traditional unilateral approach by obtaining information from senior-level public sector executives who have had substantial interaction in a mutually designed joint project. The results answer the questions of what stereotypes exist, whether "myths" exist after extensive cooperation, and what steps may be needed to promote further understanding. These questions are considered important because it has been shown that managerial attitudes and role bias are relevant antecedents of executive behavior (Sonnenfeld, 1984; Ford and McLauglin, 1984).

STUDY APPROACH AND DESIGN

This analysis of public sector attitudes parallels the study of private sector executive attitudes presented in Chapter 3. The overall approach is similar in that the same resource and BGR variables are examined in two correlation and regression analyses. However, the regression analysis reflects the variables that produced the most explanatory power for the equations, rather than using the exact variables in the resulting private sector executive equations.

Current approaches to public management and BGR require integrative, conceptual frameworks just as in the private sector to explain attitudes and decision making of public managers (Allison, 1971). Also, as in the private executive study, this analysis attempts to explore the relationships between managerial attitudes by using a resource dependence and interorganizational relations (BGR) explanatory model. For example, just as with private executives, it has been recently demonstrated that the resource dependence attitudes of private sector executives are associated with their views on BGR and interorganizational relations (Stevens et al., 1986). One further relevant question is whether and how public managerial attitudes concerning roles of government and business, resource dependence, and environmental forces act together to influence attitudes toward interorganizational and business-government relations strategies that may range anywhere from passive to conflictual.

Figure 4–1 presents the overall research design used to answer the questions about whether the attitudes of these informed managers are associated with their perceptions of ongoing or potential approaches to business-government relations strategies. The analysis focuses on how public managers perceive relations between business and government and proceeds in two phases. Phase 1 examines the issues of how resource dependence measures are related to interorganizational strategies, which range along a continuum from relatively passive consultation to directly opposing government if profits are affected, similar to the analysis in Chapter 3. Phase 1 focuses on resource dependence relationships and Phase 2 examines the effect of resource dependence in the context of other competing attitudes. That is, these informed, experienced public executives were asked in several ways to assess BGR. Phase 1 examines the associations between their related attitudes on roles, resources, and environment. The propositions under review are that these public man-

Figure 4–1
Research Design for Study of Public Managerial Experience and
Attitudes as Antecedents of Business-Government Relations
Strategies

Phase 1   Phase 2

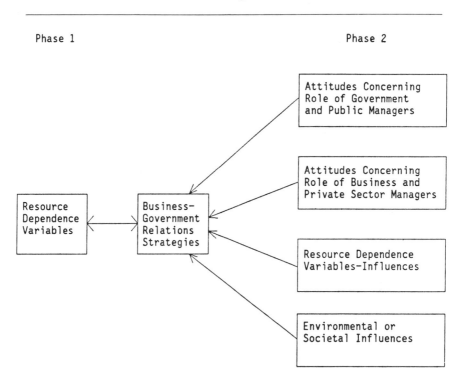

agers will exhibit attitudes toward BGR that will inform the study
and understanding of the public managerial role, especially in
regard to relationships between business and government.

RESEARCH METHODOLOGY AND PROCEDURES

To examine the questions and propositions related to BGR, the
same ten resource-based variables applied to the private executives are used. The resource-based variables include those with
explicit linkages to resource-relevant issues. The business-government relations measures include both potential and actual
strategies that have been or could be used. The overall categories
of interorganizational or business-government relations are not

designed to be exhaustive, but rather representative of realistic overall attitudes and alternatives. They are cooperative (passive, active), co-optative, negotiative, competitive, or conflictual. These strategies were derived from both the recent literature (see, for example, Stevens et al., 1986) and interviews with involved private and public managers.

The study included as respondents those top-, mid-, and operational-level public sector managers who were the governmental co-consultants in the Governor's Management Improvement Program (GMIP), which included top-level private sector and public sector managers in New Jersey. As described earlier, under the aegis of top-level state officials, including the governor and cabinet secretaries, and top-level corporate/business managers (corporate board members, presidents, vice presidents), this cooperative program to improve the management of major state functions was instituted.

There were more than 160 top-level state executives involved in the joint cooperative project at different levels (e.g., some provided direct administrative support to the governing board and did not have hands-on experience in the actual management analysis or problem resolution phases of the public agencies). Out of the overall group, 114 usable responses (74 percent) were obtained, either through interviews or through structured questionnaires. Given that a similar study of public managers has never been performed, this unique group of experienced executives is considered a noteworthy group to use in examining BGR issues that have not been previously investigated.

Represented in the group of respondents were state cabinet officers, agency heads or directors, department heads, and operational managers from 20 state agencies. Further, these executives had an average of 5–1/2 years' experience in their respective positions and more than 18 years in the public sector. Taken together, these upper-level executives exhibited intensive public and business-government relations' experiences. When combined, these individual and experimental attributes make this unique group well informed about the questions being addressed here.

Because the theoretical and empirical literature in this area of business and government relations is especially limited, this study of public executives attempts to formulate as much as to ask questions or test hypotheses. There are no prescribed methodologies or accepted individual or aggregate variables; therefore, the approach here is to disaggregate prior descriptive models into the various testable and theoretically based resource dependence, BGR, and interorganizational measures. To operationalize the relevant concepts associated with the resource and interorganizational concepts, the public managers were asked the same questions as the private executives concerning business-government relations, government and private sector efficiency, effectiveness, regulations, policy, and ways to improve business-government relations. Similarly, a 5-point Likert scale (1 = strongly disagree to 5 = strongly agree) was used for each measure/item. The resource-based, interorganizational, and BGR strategy questions were embedded within these general categories so as not to identify the underlying premises or concepts being tested or to elicit a response set. Zero-order correlations were used to investigate the phase 1 relationships, and multiple-regression equations were used to examine phase 2 of the design shown in Figure 4–1.

RESULTS

Resource Dependence and Interorganizational/Business-Government Relations

Table 4–1 presents the zero-order correlations for the resource dependence (RD) and interorganizational relations measures. The overall pattern of associations is mixed, but certain consistencies in the statistically significant correlations do emerge. For example, six of the RD measures exhibit numerous significant relationships across the general categories and 20 measures of strategy. The strongest (eight or more significant correlations) RD variables that exhibit associations with the interorganizational relations measures are business should provide resources for society, private sector cooperation determines effective resource use, societal demands deplete private sector resources, and public policies should require joint business-government fundings. Two other correlates (six statistically significant associations), government policies create competitive advantages and govern-

Table 4–1
Zero-Order Correlations Between Resource Dependence and Interorganizational Relations Strategy Variables for Public Managers[a]

Resource Dependence Variables (RD)	INTERORGANIZATIONAL RELATIONS STRATEGY VARIABLES (IORS)								
	Cooperative								
	Passive			Active					
	Business Should Consult With Government	Let Business-Government Relations Evolve	Business Follows Spirit of Public Law	Business Should Regulate Self	Improving Society is in Self Interest	Integrate Public Responsibility in Strategy	Business Establish Own Standards	Activity Promote Business Government Relations	Spread Positive Word on BGR
Government Depends on Business for Resources	.03	.06	.07	.06	−.17*	.07	.08	−.14	.01
Societal Demands Deplete Private Sector Resources	.04	.19*	.04	.01	−.30***	−.29***	−.12	−.14	−.19*
Government Reduces Resources for Economic Development	.21*	.05	.12	.12	.03	−.03	.07	.06	.11
Government Policies Create Competitive Advantages	.11	−.07	.06	.22*	.04	.21	.23*	.06	.15
Government Managers Use Resources Efficiently	.08	.01	.21*	.01	.06	.13	.01	.03	.06
Government Intervention Decreases Business Efficiency in Resource Use	.04	.11	.04	.04	.35***	.23*	.01	.03	−.26**
Business Should Provide Resources for Society	.15	−.25**	.01	.11	.38***	.53***	.35***	.09	−.27**
Public Policies Require Joint Business Government Funding	.37***	.05	.16	.01	.17	.22*	.19*	.07	.24**
Private Sector Cooperation Determines Effective Resource Use	.32***	.09	.02	.01	.10	.25**	.28**	.17*	.29**
Government Policies Must Reflect Resources Scarcity	.28**	.06	.01	.07	.07	.23*	.06	.01	.13

[a]*p ≤ .05; **p ≤ .01; ***p ≤ .001

Table 4–1 (continued)

INTERORGANIZATIONAL RELATIONS STRATEGY VARIABLES (IORS)										
Cooperative / Active			Cooptative			Negotiative Joint		Competitive		Conflict
Follow-up on Cooperation Efforts	Private Sector More Responsive	Proactive in Helping Government Problems	Private Representatives in Government Decisionmaking	Government Representation in Private Decisionmaking	Involve Interest Groups in Decisionmaking	Government Regulations Should Require Cooperation	Third Party Negotiations	Business Should Get Involved Politically	Business and Government Operate in Self Interest	Government Should be Opposed if Profits Affected
.16	.04	.14	.01	−.11	.03	.13	−.13	.33***	.29***	.31***
−.16	.14***	−.31	−.01	−.04	−.24**	.09	−.18*	.13	.13	.23*
.02	−.01	−.17	.10	.03	−.41***	.01	.09	.04	−.06	.06
.31**	.07	.01	.10	.02	.23*	.10	.18*	.18*	.11	.08
.09	.24**	.22*	.08	.03	.01	.03	.12	−.01	.05	−.05
.01	.20*	.35***	.14	−.09	.21*	.11	−.02	.06	.10	−.05
.31***	.06	.58***	−.03	.15	.22*	.10	.02	.06	−.20*	−.20*
.02	.07	.05	.28**	.21*	.02	.34***	.27**	−.04	.09	.06
.26**	.30***	.16	.29**	.08	.20*	.08	.26**	.16	.02	.09
.17*	.19*	.05	.15	.05	.17*	.01	.08	.10	−.08	.03

[a]$*p \leq .05$; $**p \leq .01$; $***p \leq .001$

ment intervention decreases business efficiency in resource use, also create an interesting pattern of relationships that illuminate some of the complexity inherent in BGR. The positive and negative relationships suggest a multidimensional, somewhat contradictory attitude set. These attitudes appear to have serious implications for the relations between business and government from the perspective of the public manager.

Two of the strongest RD variables were, business should provide resources and private sector cooperation, recognize that the interdependence between government and business is a two-way street. Business is viewed as an active partner (or competitor) that has a social role and, by reacting cooperatively or competitively, can influence how effective resources are allocated to the efficiency component of business-government transactions and interactions. For instance, the strongest positive correlations suggest that the government managers believe that if business managers were proactive in helping with joint B-G problems, improving society in their own self-interest, establishing internal standards, and integrating the public responsibility function into corporate strategy, resources would not be wasted in pursuing competitive strategies. Three of the significant negative associations illustrate that these managers do not support a laissez faire or competitive/conflictual approach to BGR. Other significant positive correlations suggest that to use resources more effectively, business should consult with government to help improve government operations, regulations should require cooperation, positive outcomes between business and government should be openly discussed, the private sector is more responsive to the public (than are government managers), third party negotiations are acceptable strategies, and business should get involved politically.

As can be seen by some of the positive correlations and many of the negative, especially for the second RD variable, there appears to be a general view that too many societal demands may deplete private sector resources. These results correspond to certain of the private executive attitudes presented in Chapter 3, and indicate that the public manager respondents here do not unanimously infer that business-government cooperation is the only answer to reciprocal relations. However, certain of the associations show that those managers who believed that many societal demands deplete private sector resources also did *not* support the following propositions: improving society is in the self-interest of business, public responsibility functions should be integrated with business strategy, business should be proactive in helping government, business should spread the word on positive BGR, interest groups should be involved in corporate decision making, and third parties should be involved in resolving BGR disputes. The positive correlations for the societal demands variable also suggest that the managers may perceive that too many pressures may be a basis for letting BGR evolve and having business oppose government if profits are affected. The "government depends on business for resources" variable also indicates that improving society may not be in the self-interest of business and that competitive postures (business getting involved politically, operating in own self-interest) and conflictual approaches (actively opposing government) are feasible BGR strategies.

Generally the correlation analysis supports the premise that these public managers strongly believe that business should be more proactive in providing resources for societal objectives, developing internal standards, and deriving strategies and methods for dealing with society and government. However, in contradiction, there is evidence that those public executives who perceive that many demands emanate from society may also believe that business is justified in not responding to all of the pressures and in operating in its own self-interest by directly opposing government. Given these counterintuitive, somewhat contradictory findings, the remaining task in this study of public managers is to move beyond this general set of bivariate associations, using a multivariate approach to understanding what factors may be related to the BGR attitudes of these public managers. The findings are addressed in more detail in subsequent sections of this chapter.

Predictors of Attitudes on Business-Government Relations

To further develop understanding about public managerial attitudes toward BGR, eight multiple-regression equations using business-government strategies or approaches as dependent variables were analyzed in phase 2 of the study. The independent variable categories depicted in phase 2 of Figure 4–1 were attitudes toward the role of government/public managers, roles of business and private sector managers, resource dependence, environmental or societal influences (industrial policy, regulation, etc.). The approach used in the analysis was to derive measures from an antecedent correlation analysis for inclusion in the regression equations. The BGR strategies were chosen using the patterns of strongest explanatory power and to represent the various alternatives and categories available or used in the instrument. One of the relevant objectives here is to examine the role of resource dependence variables while statistically controlling for the effects of other contextual influences.

The results of the regression analysis presented in Table 4–2 show that the degrees of variance explained in the analyses for the eight dependent variables were all statistically significant, at least at the $p \leq .001$ level. The levels of variance accounted for the range from 21 percent to 43 percent, with five equations exhibiting almost 30 percent or more. The other interesting findings were that public managerial attitudes toward the roles of government/public managers and the private sector managers were the most visible predictors. There were also four resource and four political, environmental, and societal measures that entered the predictive equations strongly. One other noteworthy general finding was that two variables, business managers consider the public in their decision making and too many demands on business deplete its resources, were predictors in six and four of the equations, respectively. Seven variables entered as predictors in two regressions.

The coefficients of the predictors and their relative weights validate the previous correlation findings in phase 1. They show that if business is thought to consider the public in decision making, then BGR strategies (e.g., business providing resources, developing standards, integrating responsibilities with strategies, government requiring business to cooperate, improving social conditions in self-interest, and spreading positive information on BGR) were positively influenced. Conversely, if the executives agreed that society generates too many demands, four of these same BGR approaches were negatively influenced. Other results

Table 4–2
Summary of Regression Results for Public Sector Managerial Attitudes on Business-Government Relations Strategies[a,b]

Business-Government Relations Strategies-Approaches	ANTECEDENT MANAGERIAL ATTITUDES AND FOCI											
	Attitudes Concerning Role of Government and Public Managers											
	Depth of Involvement in Improving B-G Relations	Government is Responsible for Social-Equity	Alternatives to Regulation Should be Developed by Government	Public Policies Address Critical Societal Needs	Criticism Undermines Government Effectiveness	Government Should Facilitate Business Needs	Government Output is Difficult to Evaluate	Government Decisions are Too Centralized	Government Managers are Technically Competent	Government Can Determine Which Industries Need Support	Government Should Guarantee Loans for Some Businesses	Government Experience in Facilitation of BGR's
Corporations Should Provide Resources for Societal Objectives	.13	−.27	−.17									
Corporations Should Integrate Social Responsibility With Strategic Management		−.17		.17	.19							
Corporations With Internal Standards are Less Likely to be Regulated												
Business and Govt. Managers Treat Each Other as Adversaries					.11					−.13		
Govt. Should Require Business to Develop Cooperative Approaches						−.21	−.18	−.18	.24	.11		
Business Managers Should Realize that Improving Social and Economic Conditions is in Self Interest	.19											
Business-Govt. Relations Should be Allowed to Evolve on Their Own					.21						−.15	
Business Managers Should Spread the Word When They Have Positive Relations with Govt.												.16

[a]* = p ≤ .05; ** = p ≤ .01; *** = p ≤ .001
[b]Standardized coefficients are used to identify the relative contribution of each variable.

84

Table 4–2 (continued)

ANTECEDENT MANAGERIAL ATTITUDES AND FOCI

																Summary Statistics
Attitudes Concerning Role of Govt. & Public Managers		Attitudes Concerning Business and Private Sector Managers						Resource Dependence Variables				Political, Environmental and Societal Influences				
Government Helps Economy With Fiscal Policies	Government Managers are Impartial	Business Considers Public in Making Decisions	Business Managers are Not Accountable to Public	Shareholder Wealth is Primary Business Objective	American Management Systems are Outdated	Business and Government Should Operate in Self Interest	Business Should Influence Administrative Agencies	Public Policies Must Reflect Scarce Resources	Government Policies Create Advantages for Some Businesses	Too Many Demands on Business Deplete Resources	Government Intervention Decreases Business Efficiency	International Influences Will Create More Policies	Aging Industries Need Government Support to Survive	A National Industrial Policy is Needed to Compete Internationally	Politicians are Always Running for Office	R^2 / F-Value
		.23	.21							−.23						.38 / 8.57***
		.21						.17		−.23						.30 / 6.94***
		.27		.19	.21							.17	−.19			.31 / 7.42***
	−.30														.15	.25 / 5.86
		.48														.43 / 12.5***
.23		.24	.16							−.24						.27 / 7.41***
					.34	−.13										.21 / 6.88***
		.16			.32					−.11	−.16			.18		.29 / 6.61***

a* = p ≤ .05; ** = p ≤ .01; *** = p ≤ .001
bStandardized coefficients are used to identify the relative contribution of each variable.

85

that relate to the government requiring business to cooperate show three negative influences. They were government should facilitate business, government output is difficult to evaluate, and government decisions are too centralized. Other negative predictors of different strategies (government is responsible for social equity, alternatives to regulation should be developed, government managers are impartial, government can determine which industries to support, and government should guarantee loans) suggest some equivocation about the effectiveness and roles of government in the minds of these public executives. Another interesting relationship is that the depth of executive experience and facilitation of BGR in the past positively influence two BGR approaches. These final results suggest that the public managers believe that positive, proactive postures should be taken by business executives in dealing with government-business interactions.

DISCUSSION AND SUMMARY

Generally the regression results for these public managers support the correlation analyses in suggesting that these informed managers with BGR experience expect that business managers should take a more proactive, positive approach to society and BGR, including the contribution of resources and development of internal strategies/standards. A complicating orientation discovered here is that multiple social demands are perceived as depleting corporate resources. Further, in the minds of these public executives, there appears to be equivocation about whether government alone is responsible for equity and social needs. According to the results here, the role of government in facilitating (as opposed to regulating) business and guaranteeing loans, and the complex evaluation of government outputs, along with the effects of centralized government decisions, appear to require clarification. One relevant question is how public managers can balance their responsibilities to the public, their own roles, and business-government relations.

On one level there is no controversy (i.e., government managers should be "neutrally competent" in administering the law), but on another plane the comprehensiveness, applicability, and specific pertinence of the law could be questioned, given the complexity of many regulatory, economic development, or social control situations encountered by public managers. Is government facilitation of business objectives automatically wrong or correct? Can government managers really determine which industries/corporations should receive loans/protective tariffs? What are the roles of business and government when working together?

A major question of sufficiency enters the argument about BGR because most reasonably informed people would see the benefit of business providing resources for meeting social-equity needs, but a critical question is how much is enough? Are social needs infinite, and could they divert critical resources from a prime mover in the national economy? Business executives may have indirectly or explicitly decided that government is a "cheap" moderator of multiple social demands. Conversely, public executives may not see government as an effective regulator or adjudicator of societal needs and intentions in relation to business social responsibilities. One important issue is whether either sector has the individual or combined capacity to meet societal needs.

In this area of relationships between government and business, it appears that government is expected to have the role of addressing certain market failures, such as negative externalities (e.g., unemployment, pollution, non-competitive industries). However, what is not clear is whether government alone has the mandate, resources, or expertise to address the substance of these issues. Is there a need for and who should guide a national industrial policy? Will the market adjust effectively to the national and international competing demands? The results here suggest that there is no clear mandate in the attitudes of these public managers. The apparent dilemma is whether the existing system of BGR is so inefficient or ineffective as to exacerbate the existing or projected market failures. Another issue raised in this study is whether the business and government sectors, individually or collectively, have the resources to define and deal with the multiple, competing political, economic, and social constituencies that make claims against the business and government system. BGRs have evolved from mutual hands-off laissez faire policies to extremely complex redistribution, government loan, tariff, fraud, and deregulation or re-regulation questions that require sustained, focused attention.

The results from this study clearly demonstrate that the BGR facet of public management requires detailed, substantive definition and/or analysis. The attitudes of these informed managers, after an extensive joint cooperative effort, illustrate the ambiguity of the public executive role in relation to a major political-economic reality, business. Exhortations for mutual understanding, more cooperation, public-private partnerships, and shared goals seem anemic, given the potential harm that may result from not addressing the substantive difference issues squarely. The adjudication, coordination, regulation, redistribution, control, and general welfare-equity roles of governmental managers are not clear in relation to the requirements of BGR.

Implications for Public Managers

The findings from this study of top-level state executives who cooperated with top-level corporate managers in the extensive GMIP project suggest that the role of public managers, especially with regard to relations between government and business, requires extensive analysis, consideration, and consolidation. The results here indicate that these public managers expect a more proactive, social responsibility role from business, but at the same time they feel that government may not be efficient or that too many demands may deplete business resources. To derive acceptable BGR strategies and deal with the mixed set of competing priorities, realistic models of the public management role have to be developed in the profession and within the disciplines contributing to the profession. Because resource problems and conflicting roles are the major dilemmas facing government at all levels, and the private sector is the primary source of revenue for meeting public good responsibilities, answers for resolving the issues will have to be, at a minimum, bilateral in nature. Neither the public sector nor the private sector by itself has the resources to reduce the magnitude of the problems that are government, business, societal, ideological, and legislative in content.

The study findings also suggest that the concept of public management has to be improved to encompass more systemwide multilateral perspectives that go beyond the traditional politics-administration dichotomy. This should be achieved by addressing substantive interactions, such as the business-government relationship. Neutral competence, adaptability, and flexibility are certainly desirable characteristics for public managers, but they beg the issues of proportionality and substance in specific situations, such as BGR.

The dilemma of how to effectively structure BGR is a component of the larger question of what a public manager is. This perplexing issue does not exist to the same degree in the private sector, where objectives are much more specific and short term. However, this conundrum does not detract from the responsibility that practitioners, academicians, other governmental experts, and politicians have to the whole public interest.

It appears that the complexity of the BGR sphere mirrors the ambiguity inherent in defining the role of government and the responsible public manager. However, the consequences of default for the public manager are much more visible, protracted, and irrevocable. The results of this study suggest that cooperation by itself is not a sufficient process to improve the relationship between government and business. They also illustrate that public managers have the dual responsibility of informing not only themselves, but also the private sector executives with whom they cooperate, regulate, compete, consult, or negotiate. The governmental roles of adjudication, coordination, and even control of the BGR transaction require informed public managers to understand the political-economic-social-technical dimensions of their role in relation to increasing important system needs. The results here suggest that many more analysis and mutual problem-solving approaches have to be developed to build the now ambiguous knowledge based related to BGR.

CHAPTER 5

A Comparative Perspective on Public and Private Managerial Attitudes Relating to Business and Government Interdependence

It is hard to imagine any business man saying today, as Calvin Coolidge did in the 1920s, that the business of America is business or, as Charles E. Wilson did in the 1950s, that what is good for General Motors is good for the country. If one examines the standard statements of business leaders today, one finds a plaintive argument to the effect that what is good for business may not necessarily be bad for the country. And whenever businessmen do speak up for themselves, they are rarely able to find arguments that are a match in sophistication for those of their critics or rhetoric that is equally persuasive.

NORMAN PODHORETZ
"The New Defenders of Capitalism"
Harvard Business Review

COMPARATIVE PERSPECTIVES ON COMMON ISSUES

This chapter provides a comparative perspective on private sector and public sector management attitudes relating to business, society, regulation, industrial policy, and approaches to business-government cooperation. Chapters 3 and 4 presented correlation and regression analyses separately for private and then public managers. The intent here is to make direct comparisons, using the public and private managerial responses to the same questions. Because the background and conceptual issues have been outlined in the previous chapters, it will only be briefly restated here that more than 350 top-level private and public

Figure 5–1
Framework for Examining Mutual Experience-Based Public and
Private Sector Managerial Attitudes Toward Business-Government
Relations

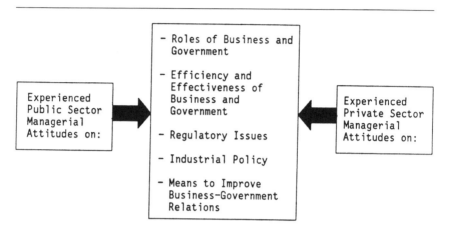

managers participated in the project. Of the approximately 190 corporate executives, 168 had direct hands-on experience and 160 public executives participated. Seventy-eight (46 percent) of the private and 114 (71 percent) of the public executives who were either interviewed or responded to a structured questionnaire were included in the comparison. Figure 5–1 represents the overall comparative framework that was used to examine the managerial attitudes. The comparison proceeds in two distinct phases. Phase 1 makes direct agree-disagree comparisons for the two groups of managers in Table 5–1A through 5–1E. The examination addresses the responses in terms of support or opposition for the principle, statement, or proposition being reviewed.

In contrast to this initial qualitative interpretation, phase 2 is somewhat more quantitative, to assess common dimensions in attitudes. It approaches the comparative framework from the perspective of common dimensions or factors underlying the managerial responses to regulation, industrial policy, and business-government relations. This perspective is considered important because thus far in the analysis only private analyses and inferential comparative statements have been made. An implicit dilemma is assessing whether there are important common dimensions or differences in managerial responses to the same questions or issues. To arrive at resolutions to opposing positions or ambiguous problems, there should be some form of comparative evolution. One objective of this chapter is to develop a framework that is oriented toward solutions using a common foundation.

RESULTS

Direct Comparisons Across Responses

Some of the comparative results of the managerial survey are presented in Tables 5–1A through 5–1E and 5–2A through 5–2J. In each table the responses of the business managers (B) and the government managers (G) are directly compared. To facilitate the comparisons, the responses for each group (B and G) are first aggregated into three categories: those who either "Disagreed" or "Strongly Disagreed" with the statement, those who either "Agreed" or "Strongly Agreed" with the statement, and those who recorded either no response or a neutral response to the statement. Then the following additional descriptors for the comparisons are used: (a) if the percentage of the group that "Agreed" or "Strongly Agreed" is greater than 75 percent, then the descriptor is "Strongly Supported"; (b) if the percentage of the group that "Agreed" or "Strongly Agreed" is greater than 50 percent, but less than 75 percent, then the descriptor is "Supported"; (c) if the percentage of the group that "Disagreed" or "Strongly Disagreed" is greater than 75 percent, then the descriptor is "Strongly Opposed"; (d) if the percentage of the group that "Disagreed" or "Strongly Disagreed" is greater than 50 percent, but less than 75 percent, then the descriptor is "Opposed"; and (e) if neither the percentage of the group that "Disagreed" or "Strongly Disagreed" exceeds 50 percent, then the descriptor is "Split."

Using these descriptors, the data in Table 5–1 show the statements in which the responses of both groups, business and government managers, were the same (i.e., both groups "Strongly Supported," "Supported," "Split," or "Opposed" a statement. The two groups did not at the same time both "Strongly Oppose"

Table 5-1
Points of Agreement Between Public and Private Sector Managers

B = Business Managers/Private Sector Managers
G = Government Managers/Public Sector Managers

		Disagree and Strongly Disagree %	Agree and Strongly Agree %	Neutral %
A. BOTH groups STRONGLY SUPPORTED the following statements:				
Business should realize that improving the social and economic conditions of society is in their self interest.	B: G:	1.3 1.0	89.6 98.2	9.1 1.8
Business managers should consider the public interest in decision making.	B: G:	6.5 1.8	88.3 90.4	3.9 7.9
To the extent possible, corporations should provide resources that can be used for achieving societal objectives.	B: G:	3.9 0.9	76.6 86.8	19.5 12.3
Corporations would benefit by helping government to deal with community problems.	B: G:	5.2 0.9	79.6 87.8	28.2 11.4
Government policies can help create competitive advantages and make business more profitable.	B: G:	10.4 7.0	85.7 88.6	3.9 4.4
Business managers should be receptive to consultation with government managers who need to improve government operations.	B: G:	1.3 0.9	96.1 82.4	2.6 11.4
Cooperative business-government programs result in business managers developing more positive perceptions about government.	B: G:	2.6 0.9	87.0 82.4	7.8 16.7
B. BOTH groups SUPPORTED the following statements:				
Undue criticism can undermine the effectiveness of government.	B: G:	20.8 14.9	67.5 71.0	11.7 14.0
Interest groups other than business should be involved in developing public policies that affect business.	B: G:	26.0 14.0	55.8 74.5	18.2 11.4
Efficiency and effectiveness in business and government differ because government doesn't have a profit motive.	B: G:	22.1 31.5	68.9 57.9	7.8 10.6

Table 5–1 (continued)

B = Business Managers/Private Sector Managers
G = Government Managers/Public Sector Managers

		Disagree and Strongly Disagree %	Agree and Strongly Agree %	Neutral %
Government decision making bodies that affect business should include business representatives as members.	B:	19.5	68.9	11.7
	G:	14.1	68.7	19.3
Government regulations should include provisions that require business and government to develop cooperative approaches for meeting regulatory objectives.	B:	18.2	57.2	24.7
	G:	11.4	72.8	15.8

C. BOTH groups SPLIT on the following statements:

		Disagree and Strongly Disagree %	Agree and Strongly Agree %	Neutral %
Optimization of shareholder wealth is the primary objective of business.	B:	39.0	41.6	18.2
	G:	34.2	46.6	20.2
Government decision making is too centralized in top level managers.	B:	32.5	32.5	35.1
	G:	43.0	39.5	17.6
Business managers follow the spirit and intent of public policy.	B:	29.9	48.1	22.1
	G:	43.4	34.2	21.9
Business and government managers treat each other as adversaries.	B:	20.8	45.5	29.9
	G:	36.9	28.1	29.8
Managerial systems used in American business are outdated.	B:	42.9	29.9	26.0
	G:	32.5	36.0	31.6
Effective government use of resources depends on how much the private sector cooperates.	B:	31.2	40.3	28.6
	G:	28.1	47.4	24.6
Business executives are competent in evaluating government efficiency.	B:	23.4	48.1	28.6
	G:	43.9	30.7	24.6

95

Table 5–1 (continued)

B = Business Managers/Private Sector Managers
G = Government Managers/Public Sector Managers

		Disagree and Strongly Disagree %	Agree and Strongly Agree %	Neutral %
D. BOTH groups OPPOSED the following questions:				
Society makes too many demands on the private sector--demands which deplete critical resources.	B: G:	50.7 68.4	22.1 14.9	27.3 16.7
Corporate managers face high levels of risk when they make philanthropic contributions and engage in other discretionary or voluntary action.	B: G:	74.0 61.4	15.6 9.6	10.4 29.0
It is the government's and not business's responsibility to carry out social service and equity programs.	B: G:	58.4 64.9	22.1 23.7	19.5 11.4
Business-government relations do not need conscious direction and should be allowed to evolve on their own to address whatever issues emerge.	B: G:	68.8 71.9	10.4 11.4	18.2 16.7
Every public policy that effects business should have a public-private partnership clause that requires the policies to be jointly funded.	B: G:	61.9 50.0	9.1 21.0	27.3 29.0

E. BOTH groups STRONGLY OPPOSE. I note:
    none of the questions were
    simultaneously strongly opposed by
    both groups.

Table 5–2
Points of Disagreement Between Public and Private Sector Managers

B = Business Managers/Private Sector Managers
G = Government Managers/Public Sector Managers

		Disagree and Strongly Disagree %	Agree and Strongly Agree %	Neutral %
A. PRIVATE sector managers STRONGLY SUPPORTED and PUBLIC sector managers SPLIT on the following statement:				
Private sector managers are more responsive to their consumers/clients than government managers.	B: G:	9.1 43.0	77.9 48.2	11.7 8.8
B. PRIVATE sector managers SUPPORTED and PUBLIC sector managers STRONGLY SUPPORTED the following statement:				
Corporations should thoroughly integrate the social responsibility function into strategic management.	B: G:	14.3 6.1	67.5 76.3	18.2 17.5
C. PRIVATE sector managers SUPPORTED and PUBLIC sector managers SPLIT on the following statements:				
Society asks too much of government for social services, thereby reducing available resources for economic development.	B: G:	10.5 34.2	66.3 43.9	23.4 22.0
Government organizations should be facilitators not regulators of business.	B: G:	19.5 29.8	63.7 41.2	16.9 28.9
Regardless of the intent, government intervention decreases business efficiency in using resources.	B: G:	14.3 38.6	58.5 41.2	26.0 20.2
To protect their organizations and business, business managers should become more involved in politics.	B: G:	16.9 35.1	66.2 39.4	16.9 25.4
Business decision making methods are more efficient than government.	B: G:	7.8 34.2	74.1 41.2	18.2 24.6
Government managers influence business more than business managers influence government.	B: G:	16.9 38.6	64.9 34.2	18.2 27.2

Table 5–2 (continued)

B = Business Managers/Private Sector Managers
G = Government Managers/Public Sector Managers

		Disagree and Strongly Disagree %	Agree and Strongly Agree %	Neutral %
D. PRIVATE sector managers SPLIT and PUBLIC sector managers SUPPORTED the following statement:				
Government managers are as professional as business managers.	B: G:	36.4 5.3	40.3 83.3	22.1 11.4
E. PRIVATE sector managers SPLIT and PUBLIC sector managers SUPPORTED the following statements:				
Public policies address critical needs in society.	B: G:	16.9 9.6	42.9 72.0	39.0 18.4
Government outputs are difficult to evaluate because they provide such complex social services.	B: G:	39.0 25.5	49.4 71.0	10.4 3.5
Government managers carry out public policies as impartially as possible.	B: G:	49.4 22.9	16.9 58.8	32.5 18.4
Government managers are more committed to the public interest than business managers.	B: G:	39.0 14.1	37.7 61.4	22.1 24.6
Government managers are as technically competent in their jobs as are business managers.	B: G:	40.3 14.9	41.6 74.6	16.9 10.5
External pressures, such as fiscal uncertainty in the economy, have to be present and recognized to promote cooperation between business and government.	B: G:	33.8 34.3	45.5 52.7	19.5 13.2
F. PRIVATE sector managers SPLIT and PUBLIC sector managers OPPOSED the following statements:				
The most important contribution which business can make to society is to be profitable.	B: G:	27.3 56.1	45.5 28.1	27.3 15.8
Government policies are unstable because politicians are always running for office.	B: G:	29.9 52.6	48.1 35.0	22.1 12.3

Table 5–2 (continued)

B = Business Managers/Private Sector Managers
G = Government Managers/Public Sector Managers

		Disagree and Strongly Disagree %	Agree and Strongly Agree %	Neutral %
The business community should actively oppose government agencies that reduce their profitability.	B:	37.7	28.8	33.8
	G:	57.9	20.1	21.9
Corporate decision makers face more uncertainty than do government decision makers.	B:	33.8	41.6	23.4
	G:	56.1	26.3	17.6

G. PRIVATE sector managers OPPOSED and PUBLIC sector managers SUPPORTED the following statement:

Business managers are not held accountable for their actions that affect society.	B:	53.3	32.5	14.3
	G:	37.8	58.5	8.8

H. PRIVATE sector managers OPPOSED and PUBLIC sector managers SPLIT on the following statements:

Government managers are efficient in using resources.	B:	71.4	10.4	18.2
	G:	32.5	41.3	26.3
Business and government conflicts would be resolved more effectively if neutral third party negotiators were used to settle disputes.	B:	53.3	14.3	32.5
	G:	45.6	18.5	35.9

I. PRIVATE sector managers OPPOSED and PUBLIC sector managers STRONGLY OPPOSED the following statement:

Business and government managers should both operate in their individual self interest.	B:	66.3	19.5	14.3
	G:	79.0	14.1	7.1

J. PRIVATE sector managers STRONGLY OPPOSED and PUBLIC sector managers SPLIT on the following statement:

Corporations should have government representatives on their boards of directors.	B:	80.6	2.6	14.3
	G:	47.4	22.8	22.8

any of the statements.) The data in Table 5–2A through 5–2J show the statements in which the groups differed. Some of the differences in Table 5–2A through 5–2J are matters of degree only, since one group may have, for example, "Strongly Supported" a statement that the other group merely "Supported," but there are some matters of significant difference as well.

Points of Agreement

An examination of the data in Table 5–1 reveals the points where there is consensus between the group of private sector managers (B) and the group of public sector managers (G). The data in Part A reflect strong support from both groups about such matters as business having an important role to play in society, business decision makers being constantly aware of that role, and active involvement of business in the public policy arena benefiting both business and government.

The data in Part B show mutual support for the idea of pluralism in governmental decision making. As part of this pluralistic idea, business and government must cooperate by engaging in such practices as minimizing undue criticism of government and guaranteeing that private sector managers are included on government bodies that affect business.

The data in Part C reflect uncertainty within each group about "what is" occurring in business and/or government. On the private sector side, both groups split, for example, on such matters as whether optimizing shareholder wealth is the primary objective of business or whether business managers follow the spirit and intent of public policy. On the public sector side, both groups split on organizational matters, such as whether government decision making is too centralized. Uncertainty is also part of each group's view of business and government interaction, since there are splits about whether the two groups treat each other as adversaries, whether government needs business cooperation to be effective, and whether business managers are even capable of evaluating government efficiency.

Yet Part D suggests that there is agreement by both groups about some matters that they both oppose. For example, consistent with the data in Part A, both groups reject the idea that too many demands are placed on the private sector or that business involvement in philanthropy, etc., adds some risk to managerial decision making. They see business as having responsibilities for social service programs, and they recognize the need for direction (although not necessarily funding) of joint business-government programs.

In sum, there are several points of agreement between the private sector and public sector managers. Most of those points appear to deal with "what should be" instead of "what is," and on questions about "what is," consensus within both groups is lacking.

Points of Disagreement

As noted earlier, some of the differences in the data of Table 5–2A through 5–2J can be viewed as matters of degree only. Specifically, the questions in Parts B and I show that both groups support the idea of business assumption of social responsibility and that both groups oppose the idea that both private sector and public sector managers ought to operate in their own self-interest. On both points, government managers have stronger opinions (i.e., government managers "Strongly Support" the first statement, whereas business managers "Support" it, and government managers "Strongly Oppose" the second statement, whereas business managers "Oppose" it.

On the other hand, some of the responses in Table 5–2A through 5–2J show substantial differences in the attitudes of business and government managers. For example, private sector managers are convinced that they are more responsive to their consumers/clients, but public sector managers aren't certain that private sector managers are more responsive (Part A). Also, public sector managers are certain that they are as professional as private sector managers, and in this case the private sector managers are "Split" (Part D). Private sector managers know that they do not want government representatives on corporate boards of directors; public sector managers are "split" on this consideration (Part J). Finally, the most bifurcated view comes in terms of whether private sector managers are held accountable for their actions that affect society; public sector managers say they are not and private sector managers say they are (Part G).

The remainder of the data in Table 5–2 reflect statements in which one group "Supports" or "Opposes" the propositions and the other group "Splits." For example, in Part C, private sector managers support such ideas as (a) government managers influence them more than they influence government managers, (b) government decision making is less efficient than business, and (c) government intervention lessens the efficiency of business. As well, government is viewed as overburdened, government should be facilitating not regulating business, and business should get more involved in politics. On all of these matters the public sector managers' group is "Split."

Conversely, many of the statements that public sector managers support reflect a split in the private sector manager group (Part E). Public sector managers see themselves as committed to the public, addressing critical needs, impartial, technically competent, and subject to fiscal uncertainty. Private sector managers reveal no consensus on these matters.

Finally, there are sets of questions that one group opposes while the other group splits (Parts F and H). Private sector managers do not believe that public sector managers use their resources efficiently, whereas public sector managers are "Split" on this consideration. In contrast, public sector managers oppose the ideas that the most important contribution of business is profit making, that government policy is unstable because politicians are always running for office, that business should oppose government agencies that affect their profitability, and that corporate managers face more uncertainty than they do. Again, private sector managers "Split."

GENERAL OBSERVATIONS

The results as reviewed above might be surprising to those who believe that there are substantial differences in the attitudes of private sector and public sector managers. For the most part these data show a good deal of agreement about "what should be" the role of business in society, the role of government in society, and the role of business/government relations in American society. Where the consensus breaks down is when questions of "what is" are posed. Particularly, statements comparing the performance of private sector and public sector managers lead to disagreements in attitudes. Criteria for evaluating government decision making are also a source of disagreement. And beyond a general acceptance of increased cooperation and interaction between business and government, there is little consensus about what should be done to improve business/-government relations.

These results indicate that many of the differences in private and public executive attitudes may be perceptual and unrealistic. Normatively, there is agreement that "good" things are desirable, but there is disagreement over matters of fact. The unresolved issues are how to determine what really exists in BGR. How can perceptions be avoided to deal with the reality of resource interdependence and the results of conflicts or competitions? If business and government want the effective relations to develop, what is stopping them?

RESULTS OF FACTOR ANALYSIS—COMMON DIMENSIONS AND STRUCTURAL ACCOMMODATION?

To produce identical, comparable patterns for the public and private managers, principal components factor analyses with varimax rotations were used to derive independent dimensions across certain measures. For this exploratory study, the relatively conservative ratios of cases to variables of at least 7.8 to 1 for the business and 11.4 to 1 for the public managers were used. To maintain consistency and comparability, ten identical items and procedures were used for both groups of managerial respondents for each category of responses. These items were chosen because they represented contemporary concepts in regulation, industrial policy, and BGR, and complement the preceding comparisons. Coefficient alpha estimates of reliability were used to assess internal consistency of the dimensions. The following three tables present the results of the analyses for the business and government managers across common items for regulation, industrial policy, and BGR strategies.

Dimensions of Regulation: Private and Public
Executives

Ten common items assessing the attitudes of business and government managers toward government regulation of business were analyzed, and the results are presented in Table 5–3. The analysis for the business managers resulted in a two-factor solution, accounting for 47 and 25 percent of the variance. Factor I with three items (over a .5 factor loading—labeled here as Proactive Political) defines a dimension that includes a proactive posture toward the executive, legislative, and government agency components of the public policy environment. Factor II with two items (Regulation Scanning and Identification) illustrates internal (in-house counsel) and external (consultants) scanning methods for identifying relevant regulations. With the respectable reliability coefficients of .72 and .74, these dimensions represent a proactive, broad, co-optative intelligence-gathering perspective with regard to the major components of the government regulatory system. Given that these high-level executives just completed an extensive cooperative effort with government officials, the strategic question of how much cooperation results from mutual understanding or partnership approaches is raised. A more complex question is what the long-term consequences are of the private sector using proactive, co-optative strategies to defuse public policies.

An interesting and noteworthy adjunct to these private sector regulation dimensions that lends credibility and validity to the preceding results is that essentially the same factor solution was produced for the government executives, the only exceptions being that direct contact with the agency was not included in the first factor solution and the higher reliability coefficient for the political involvement dimension. The second government manager factor encompasses the internal and external regulatory system. Further, these results, with their experiential referent being recent mutual participation in a joint project, lead one to question whether there are unanalyzed structural imperatives of the political and economic context that may override less comprehensive BGR initiatives. These close-to-mirror-image-findings for the regulatory facet of

Table 5–3
Factor Analysis Results for Regulation for Business and Government Managers* (Varimax Rotation)

	Factor Loadings			
	Business Managers (n=78)		Govt. Managers (n=114)	
	Proactive Political	Scanning Identif.	Proactive Political	Scanning Identif.
Regulation Variables				
1. Business takes opportunity to formulate public policy	.07	.05	.06	.18
2. Business does cost–benefit of proposed regulations	.02	.08	-.10	-.01
3. Government often accepts business concerns in final policy	-.01	.13	-.13	-.10
4. It is government responsibility to regulate true monopolies	-.01	-.03	-.06	.04
5. Internationalization will require more government regulation	.06	.00	.09	.05
6. Business should influence policy by contacting exec.	.81	-.02	.79	.08
7. Business should influence policy by contacting legis.	.76	-.07	.87	.05
8. Business should influence policy by contacting agency	.52	.34	.16	.18
9. Business identifies regulations using in-house counsel	.10	.75	.07	.72
10. Business regulations identified by outside consultants	.06	.81	.05	.81
Eigenvalue	2.11	1.12	1.67	1.24
Variance Accounted	45%	25%	41%	30%

---

*Cronbach's Alpha Reliability Coefficient for Dimensions of Regulation.

Business Managers:	Factor I	.72	
	Factor II	.74	
Government Managers:	Factor I	.89	
	Factor II	.75	

the BGR dynamic from informed, experienced public and private executives may have serious implications for developing strategies to improve these interactions.

Dimensions of Industrial Policy

Table 5–4 presents the results of the factor analysis for the ten items used to assess the industrial policy attitudes of the government and business managers. Because an eigenvalue of 1 is being used as a cutoff here, only one factor for each group of managers was extracted. Each factor accounted for 54 and 46 percent of the variance, respectively. The business manager factor (recognition of the positive government tax and fiscal roles) reflects a private sector recognition of and reliance on public policy for important government tax and fiscal support actions. The reliability coefficient of .55 represents only a moderate congruency, and signals the need to interpret this factor conservatively. However, this dimension does represent explicit recognition of the potentially significant effect of government on business profitability, potential, and effectiveness.

The three items in the public manager factor imply that the government has the capability to determine which industries (including aging industries) require support and the perceived positive value of trade restriction to business in the long run. The low alpha coefficient of .44 for this factor suggests a cautious interpretation, but considered together with the business executive factor, there is noteworthy convergence in perceptions on the role of extensive government influence on the private sector. In terms of industrial policy/role of government attributes, these findings suggest that there may be many competing interpretations of the support versus adversarial roles of government and a lack of consensus on the intensity of government influence on business. With the areas of convergence, these results indicate that there may be an explicit recognition of the resource issue associated with BGR. That is, these two items highlight not only the need for mutual managerial accommodation given the political, economic, and international

Table 5–4

Factor Analysis Results for Industrial Policy Variables for Business and Government Managers* (Varimax Rotation)

	Factor Loadings	
	Business Managers (n=78)	Govt. Managers (n=114)
Industrial Related Variables	Govt. Fiscal Role	Govt. Support Role
1. Government should use tax policy to stimulate business	.50	.34
2. Government can effectively determine which industry needs support	.35	.54
3. Tariffs/import controls help business in long run	.14	.64
4. Government should help economy with fiscal policies	.79	.06
5. Only government should have policies for high employment	.04	.14
6. Aging industries should receive government support	.29	.50
7. U.S. need a national industrial policy	.34	.18
8. The free market is best for national economic development	.01	-.31
9. American management systems are outdated	-.02	-.04
10. Individual states should have industrial policies	.37	-.01
Eigenvalue	1.99	1.77
Variance Accounted	54%	46%

---

*Cronbach's Alpha Reliability Coefficient for Dimensions of Industrial Policy.

    Business Managers: Factor I .55

    Government Managers: Factor I .44

context of BGR, but also the resource interdependence between government and business.

Business-Government Relations Strategies

The ten items used to assess strategies for improving relations between government and business are included in Table 5–5. The results of the rotation suggest that there is one underlying dimension for the corporate and two for the government executive items. Two of the alpha estimates are moderately low, with the first one for the public managers being only .52. The underlying dimension for the business factors (52 percent of the variation) may be interpreted as active corporate social responsibility (CSR), including providing resources for society and integrating CSR into strategic management. Notably, this same dimension with an added item (corporations with internal standards are not likely to be regulated) is congruent with the first public managerial factor. The conceptual issue related to BGR as perceived by both private and public executives brings into question the role of counterbalancing managerial strategies for both the private and the public sector. If the attitudes of the business and government executives represent recognition of their CSR (and the need for internal corporate standards), what systemic or nonaccommodative mechanism is operating? That is, what accounts for active, somewhat coercive public policies, regulations, or government intervention in many corporate activities?

The second public manager factor that should be dealt with explicitly is the corporate resource issue associated with BGR. The factors illustrate the perceived financial impacts of public policies on business, and also the role of private sector cooperation. Presumably, an adversarial posture by public and private organizations is not resource efficient, and this efficiency criterion is negated by a failure of business to cooperate. Having business representatives on government policymaking or decision-making bodies may be an extension of a co-optative approach to public policy in which the financial impacts would be reduced.

Table 5–5

Factor Analysis Results for Business-Government Relations Strategies for Business and Government Managers* (Varimax Rotation)

		Factor Loadings		
		Business Managers (n=78)	Govt. Managers (n=114)	
	Industrial Related Variables	Active CSR	Active CSR	Resource Effic.
1.	Corporations should provide resources for society	.75	.87	-.05
2.	Corporations should integrate social responsibility into strategy	.78	.60	.17
3.	Corporations with internal standards are not likely to be regulated	.22	.45	.30
4.	Government policies should require cooperation	.25	.03	.21
5.	Public policies should require joint funding	.06	.15	.49
6.	Effective BGR depends on private sector cooperation	.03	.24	.58
7.	BGR's should be allowed to evolve on their own	.28	-.26	-.01
8.	Corporation Boards should have government representatives	.31	.05	.12
9.	Government bodies should have business representatives	.01	-.06	.55
10.	B-G conflicts should be resolved by third parties	.10	-.01	.35
	Eigenvalue	2.2	1.98	1.19
	Variance Accounted	52%	44%	26%

*Cronbach's Alpha Reliability Coefficient for Dimensions of BGR.

  Business Managers: Factor I   .77

  Government Managers: Factor I   .52
                        Factor II   .69

DISCUSSION AND CONCLUSIONS FOR FACTOR ANALYSIS

This exploratory, comparative study examined several under-lying dimensions of business and government managerial attitudes toward regulation, industrial policy, and strategies for improving BGR. This three-part analysis resulted in the identification of certain congruent, mutual attitudes with moderately low to moderately high reliability coefficients. The literature reports no previous research on mutual BGR attitudes of high-level executives who have cooperated in a joint business-government project. In practical and research terms, the findings presented here may have important implications for understanding certain subtle relationships between the two dominant managerial forces in BGR.

The findings illustrated that business and public managers both perceived the political-co-optative posture of business executives with regard to the public policy or regulatory dimension of BGR. This is not a value question or position, but rather an empirical perspective on the practical issue of substantive interdependence. In the society-politics-business-government system, a business strategy mechanism to reduce the impacts of certain social values and the regulatory arm of government would be to influence the legislative and executive branches, where public policy is formulated. This appears to be a rational strategy for a regulated enterprise, but may complicate the relationship when these actions are highlighted in the media or through hearsay in the more or less open forum of public policymaking. Then the legitimate question of whether the *whole* public or private interest is being served arises, and those responsible for administering public policies are required to develop counter or accommodative strategies. The dilemma for the practice of BGR is whether these apparently mutually adversarial, distrustful interactions can be improved. The findings suggest that existing co-optative strategies are transparent to the relevant actors. They also suggest that cooperative or joint approaches, by themselves, are not sufficiently comprehensive to address the underlying economic-political issues in regulation. The role and effectiveness of political co-optation or the need for selected public policies that affect business and government joint approaches requires further study.

The analysis of the managerial attitudes toward industrial policy was suggestive of a recognized business reliance on government. With corporate bailouts, massive government procurement from the private sector, natural resource depletion allowances, demands for trade restrictions from certain industries, and tax reform, there is evidence that this significant dependence is recognized by both the private and the public manager. For instance, the attitudes of the public managers indicated that government was perceived to be effective in determining policies toward business, including aging industries, and that trade restrictions were beneficial to business in the long run. This is, of course, economically arguable, but these elements of private-public mutual accommodation appear to go beyond the conservative guidelines or boundaries of the much touted free market or utopian, mutual understanding models. The existence of the mixed economy model is explicitly supported by the dimensions found here.

The apparent overlap in public and private executive attitudes does not suggest complete consensus on complex, interdependent roles, but it does indicate that there may exist a mutually recognized and accommodative role for government and business managers. The question is, or rather should be, whether these results are indicative of general public, industry, or government attitudes. If they are, what are the parameters or permissible boundaries of the optimal BGR model? If significant economic or political interdependence between business and government does exist, how should it be played out? The findings here suggest that the traditional arms-length, battling-business, or bureaucracy-bashing approach (or even combinations of these) is not adequate for addressing the substantive structure of the economic-political forces involved.

The analyses and results of the strategies to improve BGR items indicate that a passive posture with regard to corporate-societal interactions may invite regulation. The underlying dimensions for business and government managers partially explain why business may not only understand, but also *expect* regulation (what some label as invasive public policies). Even if public responsibilities are recognized by business, can they all be met? Probably not, since the texture and intensity of demands are so complex and issues-based that an efficient (or maybe not so efficient) moderator of these demands is actually needed in the business-society system. This functional moderator role is served by government. Public policies partition, label, measure, and focus the most visible demands. These policies also design response mechanisms for business, possibly more effectively than business could. Government appears to serve an accommodative function between society *and* business in a manner few other societal mechanisms could. Governmental policies are imperfect BGR system mechanisms that appear to address retrospectively failures in the economic market model and redistribute resources to deal with them. That is, business needs a moderator to resolve and adjust the level of BGR system demands. Though this mechanism may be resource inefficient, the results here suggest that prospective strategic alternatives may be perceived as costing more. Can this plausible, mutual BGR accommodation be made more effective?

The results of this exploratory comparative study of public and private executive attitudes indicate that further research is needed to razor the issues and further define relevant questions. Is business the "golden goose" for government and/or society, and is government an irreplaceable mediator? The findings here suggest that the existing B-G relationship may be more co-optative than symbiotic or cooperative, and that there has been a systematic, mutual, possibly inadequate accommodation. However, the manner in which future interdependence evolves requires valid basis for accommodation and mutual recognition of the substantive economic and political variables in the system. The findings further indicate that the mutuality of private and public interests is explicitly acknowledged, but that existing attitudinal, structural, systemic, and resource ineffective adaptation strategies exist.

Finally, based on the comparative findings presented here, it appears that a superficial cooperation posture or adherence to cherished myths about mutual understanding does not appear to have much promise for resolving the substantive dilemma of how system resource effectiveness and mutual accommodation can be attained. A major resulting challenge for students, researchers, and practitioners of business-government-society interdependence is to promote conceptual clarity by developing more field-based research, more comprehensive models or interdisciplinary theories of BGR antecedents, processes, substance, strategies, and criteria to evaluate BGR outcomes.

CHAPTER 6

The Grace Commission Controversy: An Exemplar of Nonproductive Government and Business Relations

> The Executive Committee on the PPSSCC [the "Grace Commission"] was an advisory committee chartered with the Department of Commerce under provisions of the Federal Advisory Committee Act. As such, it was supposed to have regular and open meetings, be of "balanced" composition, and have its members subject to conflict of interest standards. In actual fact, however, the Executive Committee met only four times in public, with the first meeting held seven months after the project was formally launched. Also, these meetings were essentially pro forma. As for "balance," the only representativeness in the committee's composition was a well-balanced reflection of the Standard Industrial Classification Code.
>
> CHARLES GOODSELL
> "Seeking Efficiency for the Whole People"
> *Public Administration Review*

A contemporary journal that examines timely issues, *The Public Interest*, recently addressed a critical dimension of government-society interactions that has great implications for the future of BGR. However, one shortcoming of this action has been that no substantive approach for reaching an accommodation between business and government or acceptable resolutions for defining the issues have resulted. Two recent, basic articles emphasize this disparity. They are (1) Steven Kelman, "The Grace Commission: How Much Waste in Government?" (No. 78, Winter 1985, pp. 62–82), and (2) J. Peter Grace, "The Grace Commission

Controversy: Government Waste—Any Is Too Much" (No. 79, Spring 1985, pp. 111–33). Each author presented compelling, opposing viewpoints, but both essentially concluded with (*inter alia*) attacks on each other's motives in the "war on waste" in government. Kelman highlighted multiple, unfair comparisons and procedures in the original Grace Commission report. He also identified certain inaccuracies (to which Grace, in his rebuttals, gave a qualified admission). Grace (p. 111), in a direct reclame, continued to carry the argument that "the inescapable fact is that waste and inefficiency do exist in government, and on a massive scale." As hard as one may examine these counterpoints in either the antecedent or subsequent discussions, the disquieted observer is left with no valid intellectual or practical guidelines that will promote the "public" interest. Further, this contemporary controversy was bereft of a systematic review of implications for BGR.

This chapter examines some recent data based on the Governor's Management Improvement Program (GMIP) study, and a contemporary, implicit, and explicit (different dimensions of co-consultant) cooperative model used by public sector and private sector managers. A related proposal is that more substantive issues have to be proposed and evaluated to highlight the existing inefficiencies in the bureaucracy-bashing or inquisition *type* of approach. The joint "partnership" effort to be emphasized here focused on a cooperative approach that was based on a common goal of improving state government. Neither this idea nor analysis is designed to suggest that cooperative postures are always better than hands-off, arms-length, or competitive interactions between government and business. Rather, the intent here is to propose that if there is a common goal such as improved government or economic climate involved, a more mutual resource-effective form of interaction may be needed.

BACKGROUND ISSUES

There are undoubtedly myths, some with and some without foundation, surrounding the roles of public and private managers or employees that influence mutual perceptions or engender mistrust. These perceptions have persisted at least since the times of Andrew Jackson, Woodrow Wilson, or Calvin Coolidge, who thought that government would be more effective if it was more business-like. More recently, President Reagan expressed similar views, especially in highlighting the realm of government regulation. Other related, or what some call bureaucracy-bashing, views have been variously characterized as government does not have to show a profit and is therefore inefficient; civil servants are not responsive to their consumers/public; civil servants retire on the job; government makes laws it does not follow; public employees only put in eight-hour days; and government does not have to meet a payroll. Some existing stereotypes of the private sector are that private managers have little responsibility for their products beyond making a profit; private sector employees are not accountable to society; the private manager is not as visible to a broad spectrum of constituents; private employees are not considered to be on the cutting edge of sometimes ambiguous economic or social policies; the general public interest is sacrificed to make a profit; and the "bottom line" mentality works to the detriment of society overall. One shared stereotype is that the contribution of the "other" to the public interest should be greatly improved. The Grace Commission controversy has exacerbated these problems, and fueled rather than dissipated many of these heatedly argued, mutually unproductive perceptions.

Early in the history of this dilemma, part of the constitutional and intergovernmental doctrine was that government must be an effective trustee for the whole people, to include support for the living and as yet unborn. Grace, as an individual private sector corporate executive (CEO) and head of the president's commission, has directly questioned whether government is performing this task of administering effectively for the living and unborn public, who will be bearing the gigantic future costs of current ineffectiveness and growing deficits. Still, others may question whether the Grace Commission was successful in promoting the interest of the "whole" people, as opposed to certain private sector or business segments of society (e.g., Goodsell, 1984). Sufficient questions remain concerning the benefits of privatization, deregulation and re-regulation, insider trading, "golden parachutes," foreign investments, chemical leaks, corporate bailouts by government, trade restrictions, industrial policy, and government support of aging industries to reply that more information than that supplied by the Grace Commission is needed.

It currently appears that neither the public nor the private side of the controversy has moved far beyond the initial posturing and polemics. Neither representative adversary has identified whether there are substantive issues that require resolution before such palliatives as media partnerships or "mutual understanding" are reincarnated to deal with the seriously degrading mutual myths and stereotypes. Are there substantive key elements in the separate public-private spheres that have to be understood before joint business-government relations become more effective, or the related symbology is understood? The answer being proposed here is yes—and that these central issues must be openly acknowledged by both sectors before patchwork or unilateral solutions are repeatedly attempted, with the result being further separation.

THE CURRENT STUDY

This study attempts to address one central part of the competition-conflict controversy between government and business: what roles or substantive differences may account for the mutual stereotypes and what can either or both sectors do to improve conditions for more of the "whole people." The approach taken here was to examine and compare certain of the attitudes of the top-, mid-, and operational-level managers from both private and public sectors. As described earlier, the primary difference between this and other descriptions or studies is that these managers were extensively involved in a mutually cooperative co-consultant effort with a common goal—to improve the organizational structure, efficiency, information systems, and cost control systems in state government. The joint management effort included presidents, vice presidents, corporate board members and chairs, the governor, state cabinet members, and other mid- or operational-level managers in related business and government agencies. The potential problem of conflict of interest was dealt with by ensuring that industry regulators did not work with their private sector counterparts. Other elements of the information-collection process are documented in the previous chapters. These data were obtained after the formal joint report was presented to the governor and the public by the representatives of the GMIP group.

MUTUAL EXPERIENCED-BASED GOVERNMENT AND BUSINESS PERCEPTIONS

Roles and Effectiveness

One premise driving this comparative study is that managerial perceptions resulting from extensive joint interaction in a co-operative business-government program will yield more powerful comparisons than "person-in-the-street" studies. Table 6–1 presents some of the relevant comparisons with a statistical t test of significance, which is not being emphasized here because of the focus on substantive issues and potential resolutions.

The results for question 1 in Table 6–1 suggest that mutual understanding alone is not sufficient to address the substantive reality of legitimate conflicting goals within a societal context. As expected from previous findings, the private sector executives support the facilitator role of government to a significantly higher degree than do the public managers. However, even if each group better understands the other, would the substance of this facilitator issue change? For instance, in item 1, one may conceive of situations in which the government could facilitate business (e.g., legislate import restrictions, subsidize business loans to promote economic economic development, give tax breaks for capital investment). But a related question of how much latitude should critical industries, such as transportation, defense-related, chemical, or drug companies, be given is not easily answered. Does government have a public interest or a legitimate regulator role, or is it an all-or-none question? For example, who, using what criteria, should determine whether and to what extent government regulates the nuclear, oil, chemical, defense, or automobile industry? These multifaceted issues cannot all be resolved in an already saturated judicial system.

Question 2 has obviously been answered in many ways and times in our constitutional setting, but how much business "political" activity is in the best private or public interest? The recent

Table 6–1

Comparison of Government and Business Managers Attitudes on Role, Effectiveness, and Policy Issues[1]

Business and Government Executive Attitude Focus	Attitude Means		
	Government Managers (n=114)	Business Managers (n=77)	"T" Value and Significance*
Role and Effectiveness			
1. Government should be a facilitator of business	3.1	3.7	13.[a]
2. Business managers should be involved	3.0	3.6	37.2[c]
3. Business managers follow the spirit and intent of public policies	2.9	3.4	34.9[c]
4. Business managers are not held accountable to society	3.2	2.7	26.2[b]
5. Government managers are more committed to the public interest	3.6	2.9	40.1[c]
6. Government managers are efficient in using resources	3.1	2.2	56.4[c]
7. Government services are difficult to evaluate	3.6	3.7	2.5[a]
8. Business managers are competent to evaluate government effectiveness	2.8	3.3	33.1[c]
9. Most important contribution of business to society is profit	2.7	3.2	36.8[c]
10. Business decision-making is more effective than government's	3.1	3.9	55.[c]
11. Government influences business more than opposite	2.6	3.6	41.9[c]

Table 6–1 (continued)

Policy Issues

12.	It is the responsibility of government to regulate monopolies	3.9	4.0	5.7[a]
13.	Internationalization will force government to develop more public policies	3.6	3.4	22.1[b]
14.	Concerns of business are often accepted in public policies	3.2	2.6	42.1[c]
15.	Business should influence policy by dialogue with:			
	a. executive branch	4.0	4.1	6.9[a]
	b. legislative branch	3.9	4.2	20.4[b]
	c. agency itself	4.0	4.2	12.7[a]
16.	Government can determine which industry needs support	2.9	2.6	26.8[b]
17.	Government should use tax policy to stimulate business	3.4	3.5	2.9[a]
18.	Only government can deal with high unemployment	2.6	2.3	19.9[b]
19.	Policies should require joint public-private funding	2.7	1.9	57.3
20.	Effective government depends on private cooperation	3.2	3.1	9.9[a]
21.	Business should have government representatives on their boards	2.7	1.9	57.3
22.	Government policy bodies should include business representatives	3.7	3.7	.9[ns]
23.	Business-Government relations should just evolve on their own	2.3	2.2	2.1[a]

*"t" test

a_T=2-15
b_T=16-30
c_T=31+

[1]All propositions were responded to on a 5 point scale with 1 being strongly disagree and 5 equal to strongly agree.

history suggests that there may be reasonable or legal limits to political involvement by corporate executives. The results here show that public managers are not as agreeable to the proposition as are the private executives.

For item 3, business managers follow the spirit and intent of public policies, there appears to be a split, with the business executives agreeing significantly more than the public managers. What is the evidence? Do the indictments of certain defense, financial, and other securities industries chronicled regularly in the *Wall Street Journal* over the past ten years lend support to one interpretation over the other? What is the intent, and how should the law be enforced?

Other results such as those for items 4 and 5 get to the issue of accountability and commitment to the public and society. Here the government managers believe that business is not accountable, and that they as representatives of the public interest appear to be more committed to the public. Are these perceptions valid? Recently financial-based or other private sector corporations were found to have violated laws. Do or should corporations go to jail? Can some dishonesty in the private sector be used to prove that all private sector executives are dishonest or that government employees are, therefore, more committed to the public interest? The basic substance-based differences in attitudes and behavior appear to supersede the impact of the ephemeral imagery of destructive myths or baseless stereotypes in this case.

Both executive groups tend to converge on agreeing that government outputs are difficult to evaluate (item 7); however, in contrast, business managers believe that they are competent to evaluate government effectiveness (item 8). These statements are not in themselves mutually contradictory, but do contain the essence of the "government should be more business-like" argument. The underlying question may be whether one sector is capable of producing general defense, educational, social, welfare, or other services more effectively than the other.

Is profit (item 9) the "golden goose" that provides for achievement of social and welfare goals? Or is profit a superficial, short-term substitute for multiple, system-based objectives of institutions in a complex society? When is profit seeking to the exclusion of social goals harmful, if ever? Is business decision making more effective than government (item 10) because corporate managers believe that they are more effective, or is it that their objectives are more finite and measurable? In item 11 is it true that government influences business more than vice versa, as the private executives believe? Will mutual understanding or attacks resolve the dilemma highlighted by the Grace Commission controversy? How passive can the legitimate coordination and adjudication roles of government be?

The 11 items relating to roles and effectiveness of government and business are not considered exhaustive because certainly other questions were asked of the executives, but they are representative of the underlying complexity and multiple dimensions of business-government relations. There appear to be legitimate, substantive differences in public and private institutional missions. Assuredly there are also resulting frictions when these two major societal forces confront each other over multiple, sometimes ambiguous, diverse, and many times contradictory expectations. Rather than exhortations or platitudes, public sector and private sector executive roles, objectives, and interdependencies have to be more concretely defined. Mutual, interdependent relationships may have to be expanded and understood on a contingency (if X, then Y) basis rather than with absolute statements about the roles and effectiveness of business and/or government. Clearly, each function should be better defined, especially in terms of critical interdependencies.

Policy Issues and Mutual Perceptions

Part two of Table 6–1 examines certain long-standing and current policy issues related to government and business. Overall, there appears to be convergence on some of these issues, but large differences on others. For example, both groups exhibit only mild differences on whether monopolies should be regulated (item 12), business should influence policy by dialogue with the executive branch (item 15a), government should use tax policy to stimulate business (item 17), government policymaking bodies should include representatives from business (item 23), and business-government relations should be allowed to evolve on their own (item 24). These findings indicate that there is either concurrence or only mild differences with certain *de facto* government activities where the boundaries of each sector meet. That is, the responses converge on the attitudes that are in the best interest of both business and the public. For example, they are to regulate monopolies, use tax policies to stimulate the economy, include business representatives on government policy bodies, and, not too surprisingly, a tendency to let government-business relations evolve on their own.

By themselves these attitudes appear to be internally consistent, but in contradistinction to other findings presented here. For instance, there are more differences of perceptions in whether the internationalization of the economy will force more public policies to be developed (item 13—public managers agree), business concerns are accepted in public policies (item 14—public managers agree), government can determine which industry needs support (item 16—public executives agree), the free market is best for economic development (item 19—business managers agree more), and business should have government representatives on their boards (item 22—government executives agree more than private). Public managers also agree more that only government can deal with high unemployment (item 15) and that effective government depends on private sector cooperation (item 21).

The similarities, but especially these differences in attitudes demonstrate the existence of some central concerns to the society overall and business-government relations specifically. When do international, market, financial, or balance of trade influences affect the solidity of the business-governmental-social system? Should individual businesses or even multinational business objectives supersede national goals? When are corporate objectives destructive, and who should determine this threshold? Is this a "market" failure? Are legislative bodies sufficiently responsive to the objective public interest, or will the free market produce effective solutions for the diverse elements in the system of competing influences? Clearly, the answers are not forthcoming in the ongoing controversy, which focuses more on differences than commonalities.

If government policy bodies should include business representatives, why can't turnabout be fair? The results here suggest not only that major differences do exist between the public and private sectors, but also that these groups by themselves are not necessarily internally homogeneous in outlook. For example, during the Chrysler "bailout" discussions some of the most vociferous opponents of this strategy were private executives in the business community. Conversely, some of the strongest supporters of the bailout were in government. What are the BGR dynamics of this dilemma?

Has business consistently shown the ability or motivation to deal with high levels of unemployment? What is the responsibility of business for high levels of worker displacement directly resulting from specific, ineffective business actions? If business is not responsible, is this problem automatically a government or general welfare function? Who pays the benefits? Going beyond responsibility, the findings here suggest a certain incipient ambiguity (item 18) about whether *either* sector believes that government can deal with the unemployment problem.

In general terms, the overall findings here verify that the antagonisms between business and government not only have mythical-stereotypical elements, but also, more pointedly, encompass substantial dimensions that have to be genuinely understood to derive mutually beneficial resolutions. What is the value of the conflictual-competitive approaches, such as the Grace Commission model? At this point in the area of business-government relations it appears that the battling-business or bureaucracy-bashing models are counterproductive for the public and private interest because they are unidimensional and issue evading.

IMPLICATIONS AND PROSPECTS

The information derived from this particular facet of the study of these cooperative, experienced private sector and public sector executives has several implications for improving relationships between government and business. As a beginning in this dialogue, it must be explicitly recognized that there is no consensus about what the goals, processes, or results of business-government relations should be. For instance, there is a real question about whether government should facilitate or regulate, do neither, or do both for business. If either or both, how much? In terms of regulation-facilitation, is the exemplar of the Grace Commission as a competitive-conflictual approach effective? Is it a useful demonstration of the private sector capability or role even if corporate managers can evaluate certain aspects of government efficiency? Further, the evidence derived from an effective joint project and presented here also suggests that cooperative processes do not necessarily produce consensus, agreement, or cooperation through mutual understanding processes. The findings suggest that the underlying substance and legitimate differences in roles require identification and explicit, mutual resolution before real understanding occurs.

From the analysis presented here, it appears that neither the economic, political, organizational, nor social viability of the cooperative models has been demonstrated to these business executives. It does appear, however, that the political involvement (this is operationalized in different ways) and arms-length approaches have been sufficiently rewarding to engender continuing activities. If political activity results in positive outcomes, decisions, or regulations for corporate executives, then the utility of other models, such as cooperation, co-optation, negotiation, or third party resolution, have not been made as viable by the actors in the system. In this case, it is surprising that the Grace Commission approach was instituted at all unless there were serious attempts by some of the actors to actually improve government by open forum processes. An alternative explanation for the Grace Commission could be that this process was an extension or expansion of the political model to encompass or engage additional legislative, administrative, business, and public interest actors not previously involved. Judging by the acrimony of the debate and ongoing assaults on both sides of the issue, it appears that economically neutral resource acquisition or allocation processes that benefit the whole public have not been measurably improved, thereby, in some minds, making the Grace Commission a futile attempt to scale the formidable walls of public, private, and legislative opinion, which is becoming more critical of "business as usual."

The lack of tangible or conceptual payoffs or results for certain conflictual models and the ostensible use of the political process to influence policy do not in themselves prove that negotiative, cooperative approaches would be more or less effective. However, the one criterion of effective resource allocation across the "whole" or major segments of the public requires further open examination of the problem because an optimum range of satisfactory alternatives has not been explored.

European and other business-government interdependence models emphasize cooperation or joint-negotiative processes, but the U.S. posture has been primarily adversarial. This statement is not a value comparison, but a question asking what is in the best public interest for improving resource use, given the technical, economic, international, and political variables facing the United States? What are the real costs or benefits of continuing the adversarial-political or co-optation/involvement modes of business-government relations? Can a "free" market exist if certain key segments of that market demand trade restrictions, deregulation or re-regulation, subsidies, loans, or guarantees? Can either or both business and government determine which industries need support in the public interest? Is it possible for even a benevolent government to kill off a "golden goose" if that goose is the profit motive that does not always operate in the interest of the existing and yet unborn public?

The Grace Commission controversy has not produced many tangible resource or public interest products, but it has provided a service in highlighting a major government-business-public interdependency and dilemma. One critical question remaining is whether the "public" can exploit this opportunity in its own best, whole, long-term interest?

This chapter has attempted to coalesce the issues identified in previous chapters by using a contemporary manifestation of the mutual disrespect and lack of substantive understanding of conflicting roles in business-government relations. The results indicate that palliatives, platitudes, and mutual myths are linked to but do not address the *legitimate* substantive differences in the roles of public and private managers. The lesson is that superficial models or attempts at understanding are not adequate to deal with the serious, complex, political, economic, managerial, or social questions involved in how to improve relations between government and business.

CHAPTER 7

Conclusions, Implications, and Recommendations Relevant to Cooperative, Adversarial, Accommodative, and Systemic Approaches to Business-Government Relations

Big Business is undergoing a personality crisis. Not since the Depression of the 1930s have the largest U.S. corporations seemed so much under siege....

The turmoil has revived an old debate about the essential nature of the American Corporation. Who owns it? Who should own it? For whose benefit does it exist? Should the government write new rules of ownership?

The debate isn't academic.

PETER BEHR
"Debating the Nature of U.S. Corporations"
Washington Post, January 11, 1987, p. 21

Business and government leadership, employees, retirees, suppliers, customers, shareholders, corporate raiders, legislators, and multiple other "stakeholders" are questioning the role of corporations in our society. It has been argued in several forums that U.S. corporations are not productive; nor are they responsive to the environment in which they exist. It has even been proposed by insiders such as Harold Geneen (1984) and others in *Fortune* that corporate managers are not competent overseers or accountable to their shareholders or boards of directors. The fear of hostile takeovers, pressure of international competition, and "threats" of government intervention have produced great anxiety, but corporate demands for deregulation, tariffs, mergers, and divestments hardly constitute comprehensive or foresighted strategies. An important question in the complex milieu of demands for business is how to deal with the accelerating changes in the corporate environment, especially those that are instituted or mitigated by government.

Among the major objectives of this book was the assessment of current issues pertinent to BGR by reformulating them into substantive questions that could be addressed using a managerial and analytical perspective on data acquired in a recent study. The purpose of this concluding chapter is to present what are considered to be more or less conclusive implications and recommendations that flow from this study and correspond to these objectives.

SUMMARY AND DISCUSSION OF MAJOR CONCLUSIONS

The results of the analysis presented in the previous chapters have both practical and conceptual dimensions. The general finding was that the extensive interdependence between government and business was recognized by both private and public executives, but that explicit recognition of the substantively different roles of each was not apparent. Neither were explicit, operational mechanisms identified to deal effectively with the mutually recognized interdependence. One troubling aspect of this overall finding is that the ubiquitous nature of multibillion-dollar government purchases, extent of regulation, effects of national tax policy, budget deficit influence on interest rates, and industrial policy is increasing.

Another general finding was that cooperative, negotiative, and joint resolution approaches were seen as intellectually desirable; however, the results indicated that the economic viability of these BGR strategies was not demonstrated or implemented. Several possible answers to this dilemma emerged from the analysis. One alternative explanation is based on something labeled in this study as a threshold effect. That is, the mutual dependence between business and government was recognized, but the absolute number of societal and/or governmental demands may act to saturate or swamp the strategic decision-making apparatus of the corporation or governmental unit. The findings indicated that when the threshold is approached, negative responses to cooperative BGR approaches occur. This phenomenon is important because it is precisely in times of urgency or turbulence when cooperative modes of interaction between government and business are most useful.

Another possible explanation for the lack of follow through on the presumed interdependence is the failure to understand the initiator-reactor cycle in the BGR arena. For example, it was clear that the private sector executives perceived government as too inefficient in the use of resources, but it was not clear whether they analyzed the reasons for government intervention in the first place. This point introduces the question of what causes government to intervene. Most reasonable observers would argue that government policies are not random occurrences and are usually public policy responses to problems identified in the application of a policy. Many regulations may be onerous in effect once they are formally implemented through legal and administrative processes. It also has to be admitted that the "market" failed to deal with these problems; therefore, some form of protection or regulation in the general public interest is needed. A major perplexing question in BGR is whether the actors understand their relative roles in the cause-effect cycle. Government intervention was recognized as inefficient, but the cause of this intervention apparently was not understood.

A related finding in the study was that getting involved politically for the private executives appeared to be a feasible strategy. This makes intuitive sense if one considers that the economic viability of a cooperative BGR posture was not or has not been demonstrated to the private sector executives. Political involvement in some respects short-circuits the complete public policy process and potentially derails the substantive regulatory or public interest issue. The political process may appear to work in the short run; however, the erratic and episodic nature of visible problems cannot always be anticipated, so the activation of reactive political mechanisms to deal with important or long-term pressures may be counterproductive. The political involvement approach may be one of several avenues to explore in BGR, but a more proactive strategic posture by the executive or corporation may be more effective if the political activity is explicitly recognized by others with contrary views in the public policy process. Further, the use of ephemeral strategies appears to represent an avoidance or extension of an arms-length scenario for implementing BGR.

Another inference that may be drawn from the findings is that "partnership" models or approaches require further investigation because of their focus. Partnerships for the purpose of cooperation are fine, but if other objectives such as economic development are desired, the resource interdependence issues must be resolved. With the current emphasis on industrial policy, a partnership between business and government could be subject to volatile interpretation. For example, where would the so-called Chrysler bailout, trade protectionism, or support of noncompetitive industries be classified along the cooperative continuum? The mutual resource dependence perspective requires an assessment of and focus on resource use or outcomes and effectiveness rather than only on the process of cooperation itself.

One more or less inescapable conclusion for the private sector executives is that they simultaneously possess a dual set of opposing attitudes. That is, they know that they have the responsibility and justification for improving BGR, but fail to see the need to develop explicit strategies. This failure to operationalize what tend to be valid perspectives is one of the major challenges facing those who want to improve BGR. This problem is significant because to answer this challenge, the "why" question must be addressed. With the political, economic, and international context of BGR becoming more turbulent, the "why" question also has to be more focused to assess the role of political, economic, and legal factors.

Another conclusion that can be derived from the study results is that the traditional arms-length, business- or bureaucracy-bashing, and superficial partnership models are not appropriate for resolving the system strategy dilemma. A related issue is whether either the public or private sector has the motivational, legal, economic, or intellectual resources to single-handedly derive effective objectives and design resource allocation processes for the BGR function.

Conclusions Relevant to Analysis of Public Managers

A general conclusion drawn from the analysis of the public executive data was that the public managers understood the competing pressures on private executives, but still expected differ-ent behavior. The corporate executives were expected to be more proactive toward community and social problems and take a positive stance with regard to BGR. One complicating variant found here is that the public managers also recognized that mul-tiple social demands could deplete corporate resources. This finding complements the earlier private sector result that sug-gested that too many demands saturate the corporate decision-making function.

One other conclusion that may be inferred from the analysis is that the government managers question whether the govern-ment alone is responsible for meeting social and/or equity needs. One example may be the case of major unemployment or dis-placement from the traditional heavy or smokestack industries. Who should pay unemployment compensation? How are these social and economic costs distributed throughout the system? Does the aging industry that failed to adapt pay, or should other industries and public entities absorb the costs? In this one public policy area the efficiency and equity criteria are not independent, and no resolutions are forthcoming.

The public managers appear to recognize their roles as arbiters when the marketplace fails (insider trading, fraud, pollution, an-titrust, etc.), but question whether even government has the re-sources or requisite expertise to apply. Who should guide explicit or implicit industrial policies? Do government managers or pri-vate sector executives, either singly or in concert, possess the capability to devise appropriate national economic or industrial policies? Should or can joint decision-making bodies be devel-oped to deal with the increasing system complexity? The results here suggest that neither sector alone has the total economic or intellectual resources to resolve the common problems. Further, the roles of both corporation and government are increasingly being subjected to scrutiny and demands for accountability.

Another unsettling conclusion reached from the analyses was that the BGR facet of public management is also anemic or atro-phied. The public managers are uncertain about their role, and recognize that there have been major deficiencies and ambiguities in the business-government-political interchange. The exhorta-tions for more cooperation between business and government appear underdeveloped, given the questions about substantive roles, mutual dependence, national industrial policy, international competition, and the declining industrial posture of the United States. Also, there appears to be recognition that laissez faire policies are insensitive to the resource redistribution taking place across industries and nations, with increasing social claims being made against the national economic system. There is concurrence that government has coordination, adjudication, redistribution, and regulation functions, but it is not clear to these public managers how these responsibilities merge with BGR.

In addition to the ambiguous perceptions about the role of government in BGR, there is evidence from the findings that the mixed priorities about governmental roles are reinforced by the belief that business resources can be depleted by excessive demands. The overall interpretation of this group of results for public managers is that neither the public nor the private sector has the resource, societal, or legislative capabilities to deal with the current magnitude of BGR issues.

One inference that can be deduced from the findings on public executive attitudes is that models of public management have to encompass more systemwide variables. These foci have to extend beyond the traditional politics-administration dichotomy, and precepts about neutral competence and flexibility. These principles are certainly relevant; however, they are not sufficient to capture the complexity inherent in the realm of BGR. How to structure relations between government and business is a major element in how to define what a public manager or administrator is. Currently, this same issue is not as perplexing for private sector managers because of the emphasis on more specific and shorter-term organizational objectives.

The interdependence between business and government is becoming more evident in the economic and political spheres, but the results of failure in the public sector are much more visible, widespread, and protracted and many times irrevocable. The results of the findings for the public managers indicate that more cooperative processes have to be developed, but this cooperation in itself is not sufficient to guarantee substantively valid outcomes in BGR. More informed public and private executives, who are the actors in the business-government front lines, are required to shape the political-economic-social-technical-legal dimensions of their roles.

Integrative Issues in the Results

There is ample evidence both in the literature and popular press that business and government are losing the respect of the public and many informed constituencies nationally and internationally. This is a major national problem because government and business are the dominant forces in our society. The problems and foibles of elected and appointed public officials periodically pale in the light of extensive fraud, ineptness, and malfeasance in the private sector. When these institutions stumble seriously, the impacts are economically significant. If U.S. business is not competitive, the gross national product, balance of trade, and unemployment, among other national activities, are affected. When government fails to control spending or provide economic incentives for the nation, deficits and inefficient tax structures are produced. As a counterpoint, these dilemmas appear to be visible to the executives studied here; however, the results suggest that there is a momentum in the system that perpetuates the status quo.

With the challenges to managers in both sectors, there exists a need to overcome mutual stereotypes and myths. The recent past would lead one to offer a less than energetic prognosis. The alternatives for addressing the problems center on the need to explicitly identify the substantive differences and congruencies between roles and responsibilities of the private and public sector. The current difficulties do not result from differences in ability or knowledge, but competitive and conflictual behaviors have been established and are routinely played out. Perspectives and roles tend to exacerbate the differences and bureaucratic procedures, which become embedded as anachronistic behavior. These problems are clearly systemic and not individual. It appears that these interdependencies have coalesced around adversarial or, at best, laissez faire approaches, which do not address the common problems of an international economy. Can either sector remain neutral to the other where political activation or explicit co-optative actions reduce the effectiveness of relative public interest roles?

One dilemma not clearly addressed by the results of the analysis is the level of interpenetration for each sector. It would appear from the findings that some level of business participation in forming or reformulating public policy may be appropriate, but neither the level of participation nor the extent of business involvement can currently be defined. A related question addressed in this study was the extent of government participation in private sector decision making. Neither private nor public managers supported the idea. However, there did appear to be some support for a co-participation model in the public-private relationship. A major complicating factor in interpreting the results is the difficulty in determining where the boundaries of the political and economic context begin and end. A prospective question that deserves more attention in future research is how and to what effect co-determination models can be used to improve BGR.

Other conclusions derived from the study of common dimensions were that public and private managers perceived the cooptative posture of business and that business recognized its reliance on government for bailouts, trade restrictions, and government procurement. It was also apparent that both sectors perceived government to be practicing an accommodative role in BGR, and this accommodation was recognized explicitly. The results suggest that a passive-reactive government role exists and has brought BGR to its present state, but there is no answer to the question of what level of activation may be required to balance this structure. Government policies serve the role of retrospectively redistributing resources between various "markets" to address failures, and though imperfect or inefficient, business may structurally require this type of policy moderator. An issue is whether this moderating activity is more resource intensive than more mutually derived strategies.

An integrative conclusion extrapolated from the results of the study is that the complexity inherent in the current and projected relations between business and government requires valid, consensual BGR models that identify the key resource interdependence and political parameters in the public-private policy process. Explicit acknowledgement of the issues in an open national forum that focuses on the substance of public-private sector roles, effectiveness, and regulation is required. To initiate and sustain the process, mutually beneficial business-government strategies are needed to resolve the remaining ambiguity concerning common goals and objectives. Most approaches to date have been openly adversarial and co-optative (e.g., the Grace Commission) or superficial in defining and addressing the mutual resource and substantive interdependence (i.e., limited geographic or narrowly focused "partnerships").

REMAINING QUESTIONS AND UNRESOLVED ISSUES

This study has produced various results and provided the basis for proposing specific questions, implementation approaches, and recommendations. Some of the questions that deserve further attention in research and practice are:

What are "markets" and what are their roles in BGR?

What is the "cost" of ignoring social demands?

Is there a cost for business not cooperating with government?

What is the effectiveness of co-opting the regulatory process by wielding "political" influence?

Does cooperation mean the same thing to business and government (not just unilateral consultation)?

Are private or public managerial models outdated or incomplete because they do not address the integrative nature of BGR in the social system?

Are private managers necessarily capable of evaluating and improving public organizations (e.g., the Grace Commission)?

What is the basis for the mutual stereotyping between the private and public sectors, and what should be done to prevent it?

Do private sector managers understand the public policy process?

How can successful "partnerships" be reinforced and extended to other sectors of BGR?

Would cooperative approaches make regulation more effective?

What is the payoff or opportunity costs of adversarial relations between business and government?

Are there more effective mechanisms than regulation to "persuade" business to meet its legal responsibilities?

Can voluntary approaches to BGR be made effective?

How can more comprehensive approaches to integrating pragmatic and conceptual needs be developed?

Can the costs, effectiveness, or benefits of cooperative BGR be
assessed?

What steps would be necessary to devise co-determination models
for business and government?

What accommodative roles could either government or business
develop to promote effective BGR?

What are the required elements of a research agenda to study BGR?

How can a theory or body of coherent propositions be developed
and tested?

How critical are theories to further development of knowledge in
the business, government, society, and public policy process?

What BGR actions are in the best interest of the public, business,
and government?

IMPLEMENTATION AND RECOMMENDATION ISSUES: AN INTEGRATIVE PERSPECTIVE ON BGR

Many questions remain to be answered, as demonstrated by
the preceding discussion, but there are also lessons to be derived
from the study results that pertain to implementation and follow-
up actions. A key issue in the resolution of BGR problems is the
identification of responsibility. The temporal and organizational
or decision-maker dimensions of this responsibility are especially important. This implies that key individuals and/or organizations should develop plans and/or agendas that identify the
most central BGR issues for decision makers and decision points.
Further, in the context of BGR, joint agendas that affect both
business and government should be jointly derived.

Because the relations between government and business occur
in the context of the public interest and policy, joint efforts
should include multiple constituencies and stakeholders. This
integrating approach would have the capability of providing or
deriving joint assessments and goals or objectives. Although this
mechanism does not necessarily have to include current government, public, interest group, and business executives, a timely
or substance-based exploration may make it mandatory. There

are many nationally visible individuals who have past or current private and/or public sector experience and the intellectual scope to take on such an ambitious project. A major question is how to establish a visible agenda that addresses multiple public and private system needs.

Though there may be more operational objectives for joint BGR groups, one major goal should be to coalesce the process of cooperation into an objective. That is, the emphasis should be on interdependence rather than on independence of business and government. This does not mean that either or any constituency attempts to co-opt or explicitly identify cooperative models with the other, but that the nature of the BGR task and mutual benefits be consistently highlighted. One related dilemma is how to identify which sector should take the lead in coordinating the various public, business, and government constituencies. If one side appears to be dominating the process, or if there is too much equivocation about roles and directions, the basic requirement of jointedness may be dissolved.

It currently appears that there are enough serious business and government problems to go around and attract or focus attention; however, there also appears to be a vacuum of leadership. The debate on industrial policy quickly polarizes into free market versus government interference arguments without attention to the long-term, international competitive or government-business interdependence issue. An integrative model that defines common goals and/or objectives, and most likely steps to be taken in outlining responsibilities and identifying agenda items, would go a long way in rationalizing the diverse positions and needs indicative of a complex society. A relevant framework for beginning such a dialogue would be to codify lessons from the past and link them with proactive plans or targeted studies that address untested assumptions.

A contemporary question is whether the current international trade, postindustrial transitions, and level of government activities are volatile enough to energize a joint business-government effort. Buck passing or responsibility shedding is a time-worn tradition in complex interactions, but simple authority and responsibility designations do not deal with the multiple constituencies and objectives in BGR. In the past, there have been several government-business interactions, such as the Lockheed and Chrysler bailouts, that focused attention on the interdependent relationships between sectors. The current manifestations are restrictive trade practices against Japan, Canada, and others. The international balance of trade deficits and federal budget shortfalls may be appropriate issues to focus the problem-solving capacity of national leaders. With government and business both under attack for lapses in leadership and ethics, the timing may appear to be a problem. Conversely, when there is turbulence and promises of more uncertainty, knowledgeable business, government, academic, and public executives or courageous "social" entrepreneurs may have a more receptive audience.

The arms-length and business- or bureaucracy-bashing approaches seem to have run their course and demonstrated their incapacity to deal with the substantive political, economic, international, technical, and social values' questions. In addition, there are actually too many actors in the arena and too many reasons for not attacking this historical and substantive complexity. But there is also one strong reason for doing something. The ongoing chain of events has the potential to eliminate doing anything after certain undefined system resource thresholds are passed. This may be more of a problem for those who study this issue than for those who could truly do something about it. One caveat is that the combative chair and adversarial Grace Commission posture produce more forceful and opposite reactions that do not emphasize the system resource interdependence between business and government.

The political, economic, and public contexts seem to demand integrative or forward-looking solutions, but the leadership in each sector appears to be in a retreat or in a default mode of strategy. The current state of affairs, internal system battles with no allocation of resources to strategic, common goals such as improved BGR, do not augur well for the future. This study and analysis will have served their purpose if in some way more directed energy is devoted to making improved BGR a strategic agenda item for relevant business, government, public, or academic constituencies.

SUMMARY AND CONCLUSIONS

The business-government-society system is composed of interdependent elements with mutually reinforcing or destructive roles. Each sector has the responsibility to provide questions, alternatives, and answers for solving each other's, and therefore its own, problems. This study has reinforced the findings and stereotypes derived in past studies and also demonstrated that cooperative mechanisms do provide further avenues of understanding. This suggests that partial, if not the full, processes or mechanisms for achieving answers are possible to derive. Each part of the system has been rewarded for independent thinking and action that have produced not only major economic benefits, but also long-term, serious costs. There appears to be no real alternative to joint exploration of the substantive joint roles of business and government in our world. The tendency toward specialization and fragmentation provides a counterforce oriented toward mutually defined, common, integrative goals. Top-level corporate, public, and government leaders have the perspective, and consequently the responsibility, if not the total resources, to initiate positive action in BGR.

There are serious questions about the role of corporations and government in society, and a proactive posture in helping to define this scale in the context of the government's adjudication, coordination, regulation, and redistribution functions could have beneficial effects. A national public-private symposium or study group composed of representative corporate, government, and public individuals would have the potential to develop a plan that outlined issues, priorities, and strategies to facilitate mutual problem-solving approaches to BGR. A stark current assessment would be that BGRs are as dysfunctional as ever, and that the actions by both sectors invite further degradation if some conscious, joint leadership strategy is not soon formulated.

The past history of BGR is certainly an indicator of the future, but it cannot serve as a blueprint. The principal business and government actors have to devise a preferred future state of affairs and participate in methods for achieving this hegemony among constituent government, business, and societal elements. This process should be as broad-based and open as possible to elicit the participation of the interested and affected communities or stakeholders. The mutually derived procedures could focus on defining the major BGR issues and components, the desired ends and means or alternatives for achieving those ends, the resource interdependence and allocation processes needed, the most systematic implementation steps, and some measure of guidance or control over the procedures and performance. The implementation and evaluation phases of the interactive planning or study procedure would require a consistent focus on the long-term resource and interdependence activities. The members or observers of this BGR analysis approach should also be proactive in attempting to specify ideal objectives and conditions.

A focused or national study or agenda-setting group has the advantage not only of coalescing issues, but also of identifying the demand for flexibility and adaptability to address the turbulence and heterogeneity in the BGR system. It is likely that no single structure or criterion would be developed prior to a full examination of the multidimensional environment confronting corporations and government. The process would have to define the issues in an open, democratic, and interactive exchange process in which existing or emergent interest group, intellectual, economic, political, or ideological inputs are used to fuel the intended, interactive outputs of feasible, mutually reinforcing BGR strategies. Early conclusions are probably not possible or desirable, given the long-standing and fragmented history. Creativity is required and must be further nurtured instead of seeking premature closure.

Sectors in the government and business that have the most to lose or gain from BGR have the responsibility for shaping the social-political mechanisms that have to produce a context in which few facts and ambiguous perceptions exist. The guiding or shaping of a joint private-public, agenda setting process by a knowledgeable group of nationally recognized executives is required. One preliminary step may be to derive a narrowly focused BGR agenda using the most visible, contemporary dilemmas such as the federal budget deficit or balance of trade inequality. This approach would be useful in defining boundaries, constituencies, problems and ongoing objectives. Unintended outcomes of the joint process could also be diagnosed using this type of evolutionary strategy.

One of the practical, frustrating dilemmas of BGR is that each sector has "captured" the other with accommodative, but ineffective strategies, thereby constraining itself in producing change. Accommodation to conflict and hostile competition can only lead to further degradation in the relationship where demands are escalating, resources scarce, and the options for unique, problem-focused actions reduced. The net benefits of cooperation are not easily measured or correlated to the "markets" of BGR, but among the costs of conflict appear to be increasingly disruptive relations, long-term common resource depletion, growing governmental budgets/deficits, potential mutual neutralization or destruction, and nonadaptive, global economy behavior. The potential costs of cooperation may be eventual co-optation of one sector by the other or a resulting "planned" economy, which may have negative long-term effects. Though the benefits and costs of cooperation are difficult to quantify, the costs of conflict are more visible and potentially mutually destructive because each iteration of conflict in the cycle leads to a more serious outcome.

APPENDIX

Survey Instrument Developed for the GMIP Study Program

ISSUES RELATED TO IMPROVING BUSINESS-GOVERNMENT RELATIONS

A. **GENERAL BACKGROUND** In the spaces below, please fill in the number of years for each category of service, organizational/functional experience and your present position.

1. Title of Present Position Years   _____Years in Public Sector
   (or most recent position)   _____Years in Private Sector .

2. Please list major <u>functional area</u> and <u>years</u> in that functional area (for example, marketing, finance, personnel, etc.)

   _____   _____Years

3. Please list the **major** <u>type</u> <u>of</u> <u>activity</u> you performed in that functional area (e.g., planning, analysis, administration, budgeting).

   _____

4. Please indicate below what the primary nature of your work experience with business and government relations has been:

   _____Adversary
   _____Somewhat Adversary
   _____Neutral
   _____Somewhat Facilitator
   _____Facilitator

5. To what <u>extent</u> (i.e., number of agencies or functions) have you been involved with programs to improve business-government relations?

   _____None
   _____Very Little Involvement
   _____Some Involvement
   _____Moderate Involvement
   _____Great Deal of Involvement

6. To what <u>depth</u> (i.e., involvement in managerial decisionmaking) have you been associated with in efforts to improve business-government relations?

   _____None
   _____Very Little Involvement
   _____Some Involvement
   _____Moderate Involvement
   _____Great Deal of Involvement

                   ON THE LINE TO THE RIGHT OF EACH STATEMENT, PLEASE PLACE
Directions: THE NUMBER FROM THE RESPONSES BELOW THAT MOST CLOSELY
                   CORRESPONDS TO YOUR PERCEPTIONS CONCERNING THE STATEMENT

STRONGLY   STRONGLY
DISAGREE   DISAGREE   NEUTRAL   AGREE   AGREE
    1   2   3   4   5

B.   **GENERAL ISSUES IN BUSINESS-GOVERNMENT RELATIONS**

1.   Government organizations should be facilitators not regulators of business.

2.   Business managers should consider the public interest in decision making.

3.   Government policies are unstable because politicians are always running for office.

4.   To protect their organizations and business, business managers should become more involved in politics.

5.   Business managers follow the spirit and intent of public policies.

6.   Public policies address critical needs in society.

7.   Government depends on business for many of its resources.

8.   Society makes too many demands on the private sector which depletes critical resources.

9.   The business community should actively oppose government agencies that reduce their profitability.

10. Business and government managers treat each other as adversaries.

11. Government policies must reflect how scarce resources are becoming.

12. Business managers are not held accountable for their actions that affect society.

13. Society demands too much from government for social services, thereby reducing available resources for economic development.

14. Government managers are more committed to the public interest than business managers.

15. Government policies can help create competitive advantages and make certain businesses more profitable.

16. If business regulated itself effectively, government would be less likely to intervene in business affairs.

17. Business and government managers should both operate in their individual self-interest.

STRONGLY DISAGREE	DISAGREE	NEUTRAL	AGREE	STRONGLY AGREE
1	2	3	4	5

C. **EFFICIENCY AND EFFECTIVENESS ISSUES IN BUSINESS-GOVERNMENT RELATIONS**

18. Government outputs are difficult to evaluate because they provide such complex social services.

19. Private sector managers are more responsive to their consumers/clients than government managers.

20. Government managers are efficient in using resources.

21. Government managers carry out public policies as impartially as possible.

22. Business executives are competent in evaluating government efficiency.

23. Government decision making is too centralized to top level managers.

24. Business' decision making methods are more effective than government's.

25. Efficiency and effectiveness in business and government differ because government doesn't have a profit motive.

26. Regardless of the intent, government intervention decreases business efficiency in using resources.

27. Government managers are as professional as business managers.

28. Undue criticism can undermine the effectiveness of government.

29. The most important contribution that business can make to society is to be profitable.

30. It is the government's and not business' responsibility to carry out social service and equity programs.

31. Corporate managers face high levels of risk when they make philanthropic contributions and engage in other such discretionary or voluntary actions.

32. Corporate decision makers face more uncertainty than do government decision makers.

33. Optimization of shareholder wealth is the primary objective of business.

34. Government managers influence business more than business managers influence government.

35. Government managers are as technically competent in their jobs as are business managers.

STRONGLY DISAGREE	DISAGREE	NEUTRAL	AGREE	STRONGLY AGREE
1	2	3	4	5

D. ISSUES RELATED TO REGULATION OF BUSINESS

36. Business affected by regulation appears to take every legitimate opportunity to assist in the formulation of regulatory policy.

37. Business has many opportunities to present views to regulators on specific regulatory proposals.

38. Business regularly submits its views to regulators on particular regulatory proposals.

39. Business estimates of the expected costs and benefits of regulatory proposals underlay business' support or opposition of the proposals.

40. Business economic impact analyses of regulatory proposals are regularly provided to regulators to assist in the efficient selection of regulatory actions.

41. The concerns of business are most often accepted by public policy makers in the regulatory policy finally adopted.

42. Alternatives to achieve deregulation should be considered as a major objective by government agencies.

43. The process of identifying and assessing the impact of regulatory action or proposals involves the collaboration of management with legal counsel.

44. It is the responsibility of government to regulate true monopolies.

45. The internationalization of business will force government to develop more public policies that affect business.

(46-48) Business should attempt to assist in the formulation of regulatory policies through the following means:

    46. Dialogue with the executive Branch (i.e., governor, president, cabinet).

    47. Dialogue with legislators to shape administrative agency powers.

    48. Direct contacts with the relevant administrative agency.

(49-52) Business identifies potential areas of regulatory concern by:

    49. Reading regularly published government documents.

    50. Being alerted by in-house legal counsel.

    51. Being alerted by outside consultants or law firms.

    52. Being alerted by trade associations or newsletters.

STRONGLY DISAGREE	DISAGREE	NEUTRAL	AGREE	STRONGLY AGREE
1	2	3	4	5

E. **ISSUES RELATED TO DISCUSSIONS OF INDUSTRIAL POLICY**

53. Government should use tax policy to stimulate specific business investment.

54. Government can effectively determine which industries or businesses need government support.

55. Government tariffs or import controls help business in the long run.

56. Government should help the economy to grow by using fiscal policies.

57. High unemployment can only be dealt with using government policies.

58. Aging industries should receive government support to help them survive.

59. The United States needs a national industrial policy to be able to meet international competition.

60. Individual states should develop their own industrial policies.

61. The best approach to national industrial development is the free market system.

62. Managerial systems used in American business are outdated.

63. Government should guarantee loans for some business and industries.

F. **WAYS TO IMPROVE BUSINESS-GOVERNMENT RELATIONS**

64. Businesses should realize the improving the social the economic conditions of society is in their own self interest.

65. To the extent possible, corporations should provide resources that can be used for achieving societal objectives.

66. Corporations should thoroughly integrate the social responsibility function into strategic management.

67. Corporations with established standards for meeting their social responsibilities are less likely to be regulated.

68. Corporations would benefit by helping government to deal with community problems.

69. Government regulations should include provisions that require business and government to develop cooperative approaches for meeting regulatory objectives.

70. Every public policy that affects business should have a public-private partnership clause that requires the policies to be jointly funded.

STRONGLY DISAGREE	DISAGREE	NEUTRAL	AGREE	STRONGLY AGREE
1	2	3	4	5

71. Interest groups other than business should be involved in developing public policies that affect business.

72. Effective government use of resources depends on how much the private sector cooperates.

73. Business government relations do not need conscious direction and should be allowed to evolve on their own to address whatever issues emerge.

74. Corporations should have government representatives on their Board of Directors.

75. Business and government conflicts would be resolved more effectively if neutral third party negotiators were used to settle disputes.

76. Joint business-government efforts have to be followed up on over a long time after the initial cooperation to be effective.

77. Business executives who have had positive relationships with government have the responsibility to spread the word to other executives in the private sector.

78. External pressures, such as fiscal uncertainty in the economy, have to be present and recognized to promote cooperation between business and government.

79. Business managers should be receptive to consultation with government managers who need help to improve government operations.

80. Government decision making bodies that affect business should include business representatives as members.

81. Cooperative business-government programs result in business managers developing more positive perceptions about government.

IF YOU HAVE ANY COMMENTS ON HOW YOU THINK BUSINESS GOVERNMENT RELATIONS
COULD BE IMPROVED IN THE FUTURE PLEASE COMMENT ON A SEPARATE SHEET

Your age?_____

Highest diploma/certificate/degree obtained?_____

WOULD YOU LIKE A SUMMARY OF THE RESULTS OF THIS SURVEY?   ____YES ____NO
(IF YES, PLEASE INCLUDE YOUR ADDRESS)

THANK YOU FOR YOUR COOPERATION AND TIME!!

References

Action for Children's Television v. FCC, 564 F.2d 458 (D.C. Cir. 1977).

Adams, Salisbury M. "Introduction: Performance Through Partnership," and "Public/Private Sector Relations," *The Bureaucrat: The Journal for Public Managers* (Spring 1983):6–10.

Allison, Graham T. *The Essence of Decision: Explaining the Cuban Missile Crisis.* Boston: Little, Brown and Company, 1971.

Aupperle, K., J. D. Hatfield, and A. B. Carroll. "Instrument Development and Application in Corporate Social Responsibility," *Proceedings: Academy of Management* (1983), pp. 369–73.

Banks, Louis. "The Mission of Our Business," *Harvard Business Review*, 53 (May/June 1975):57–65.

Behr, Peter. "Debating the Nature of U.S. Corporations," *Washington Post*, January 11, 1987, p. 21.

Bok, D. "The Changing Corporation," extracts from the *1979 Annual Report*, in L. E. Preston, ed., *Business Environment/Public Policy, 1979 Conference Papers* (1980), pp. 232–35.

Buchholz, R. A. *Business Environment/Public Policy.* Washington, D.C.: American Assembly of Collegiate Schools of Business, 1980.

Buchholz, R. A. *Essentials of Public Policy for Management.* Englewood Cliffs, N.J.: Prentice-Hall, 1985.

Dolan, Patrick J. "State Level Management and Productivity Improvement: A Public-Private Sector Partnership Approach," *Public Productivity Review*, 7 (Winter 1984):353–68.

Dowling, J. B., and N. V. Shaeffer. "Institutional and Anti-Institutional Conflict Among Business, Government and the Public," *Academy of Management Journal*, September 1982, pp. 683–89.

Driscoll, J. W., Gary L. Cowger, and Robert J. Egan. "Private Managers and Public Myths—Public Managers and Private Myths," *Sloan Management Review*, Fall 1979, pp. 53–57.

Epstein, E. M. *The Corporation in American Politics*. Englewood Cliffs, N.J.: Prentice-Hall, 1969.

Ford, R., and F. McLaughlin. "Perceptions of Socially Responsible Activities and Attitudes: A Comparison of Business School Deans and Corporate Chief Executives," *Academy of Management Journal*, September 1984, pp. 666–74.

Fortune. "What Managers Can Learn from Manager Reagan," September 15, 1986.

Fox, J. R. *Managing Business-Government Relations*. Homewood, Il.: Richard D. Irwin, 1982.

Friedman, M., and R. Friedman. *Free to Choose*. New York: Avon, 1979.

Galbraith, J. K. *Economics and the Public Purpose*. Boston: Houghton-Mifflin, 1973.

Geneen, H. *Managing*. New York: Doubleday, 1984.

Goodsell, Charles T. "The Grace Commission: Seeking Efficiency for the Whole People?" *Public Administration Review*, May/June 1984, pp. 196–204.

Grace, J. Peter. "The Grace Commission Controversy: Government Waste—Any Is Too Much," *The Public Interest* 79 (Spring 1985):111–33.

Gray, Barbara, and T. M. Hay. "The National Coal Policy Project: An Interactive Approach to Corporate Social Responsiveness," in L. E. Preston, ed., *Research in Corporate Social Performance and Policy*, vol. 7. Greenwich, Conn.: JAI Press, 1985, pp. 191–212.

Home Box Office, Inc. *v.* FCC, 567 F.2d 9 (D.C. Cir.), *cert. denied*, 434 U.S. 829 (1977).

Hughes, J.R.T. *The Governmental Habit*. New York: Basic Books, 1977.

Hurst, J. W. *The Legitimacy of the Business Corporation in the Law of the United States, 1780–1970*. Charlottesville, Va.: The University Press of Virginia, 1970.

Ingraham, Patricia W., and Carolyn R. Ban. "Models of Public Management: Are They Useful to Federal Managers in the 1980s?" *Public Administration Review*, March/April 1986, pp. 158–60.

Jacoby, N. H., ed. *The Business-Government Relationship: A Reassessment*. Pacific Palisades, Calif.: Goodyear, 1975.

Jones, T. M. "An Integrating Framework for Research in Business and Society: A Step toward the Elusive Paradigm." *Academy of Management Review* 8 (1983):559–64.

Kelman, Steven. "The Grace Commission: How Much Waste in Government?" *The Public Interest*, 78 (Winter 1985):63–82.

Levitt, Theodore. "Why Business Always Loses," *Harvard Business Review*, 46 (March/April 1968):81–89.

Lindblom, C. E. *Politics and Markets: The World's Political-Economic Systems*. New York: Basic Books, 1977.

McCraw, T. K. "Business and Government: The Origins of the Adversary Relationship," *California Management Review*, 26 (Winter 1984):33–52.

McFarland, D. E. *Management and Society*. Englewood Cliffs, N.J.: Prentice-Hall, 1982.

Mitnick, B. M. *The Political Economy of Regulation*. New York: Columbia University Press, 1980.

Moore, T. "The New Libertarians Make Waves," *Fortune*, August 5, 1985, pp. 74–78.

Morgan, Gareth. *Images of Organization*. Beverly Hills, Calif.: Sage Publications, 1986.

Murray, Victor V., and Todd Jick. "Strategic Decision Responses to Hard Times in Public Sector Organizations," *Academy of Management Proceedings*, August 1981, pp. 339–43.

Perry, James L., and Kenneth L. Kraemer. *Public Management: Public and Private Perspectives*. Palo Alto, Calif.: Mayfield Publishing Co., 1983.

Pfeffer, J., and G. Salancik. *The External Control of Organizations: A Resource Dependence Perspective*. New York: Harper and Row, 1978.

Podhoretz, Norman. "The New Defenders of Capitalism," *Harvard Business Review*, 59 (March/April 1981):96–106.

Preston, L. E., "Business, Society and Public Policy: Current Research and Research Approaches," in *Business Environment/Public Policy, 1979 Conference Papers*, American Assembly of Collegiate Schools of Business, 1980, pp. 232–35.

Preston, L. E., and J. E. Post. *Private Management and Public Policy*. Englewood Cliffs, N.J.: Prentice-Hall, 1975.

Provan, K. G. "Technology and Interorganizational Activity as Predictors of Client Referrals," *Academy of Management Journal*, 27 (1984):811–29.

Provan, K. G., J. M. Beyer, and C. Kruytbosch. "Environmental Linkages and Power in Resource-Dependence Relations Between Organizations," *Administrative Science Quarterly*, 25 (1980):200–25.

Rainey, Hal G., Robert W. Backoff, Charles H. Levine. "Comparing Public and Private Organization," *Public Administration Review*, 36 (March/April 1976):233–44.

Reich, R. B. *The Next American Frontier*. New York: Times Books, 1983.

Ring, Peter Smith, and James L. Perry. "Strategic Management Processes in Public and Private Organizations: Implications of Distinctive Contexts and Constraints,"*Academy of Management Review*, April 1985, pp. 276–86.

Savas, Emanuel S. *Privatizing the Public Sector: How to Shrink Government*. Chatham, N.J.: Chatham House Publishers, 1982.

Sethi, S. P., N. Namiki, and C. L. Swanson. *The False Promise of the Japanese Miracle*. Boston: Pitman, 1984.

Sonnenfeld, J. A. "Executive Apologies for Price Fixing: Role Biased Perceptions of Causability," *Academy of Management Journal*, September 1984, pp. 192–98.

Steiner, George A., and John F. Steiner. *Business, Government and Society*, 4th ed. New York: Random House, 1985.

Stevens, John M., and Robert P. McGowan. "Managerial Strategies in Municipal Government Organizations," *Academy of Management Journal*, September 1983, pp. 527–34.

Stevens, John M., Steven L. Wartick, and John W. Bagby. "Business-Government Relations: An Empirical Perspective on Resource Dependence and Strategy Issues," in *Best Papers Proceedings: Academy of Management*, edited by John A. Pearce and Richard Robinson, August 1986, pp. 326–30.

Stone, Christopher. *Where the Law Ends*. New York: Harper and Row, 1975.

Sturdivant, F., and J. Gintner. "Corporate Social Responsiveness: Management Attitudes and Economic Performance," *California Management Review*, 20 (Spring 1977):30–39.

Thompson, J. D., and J. W. McEwen. "Organizational Goals and Environments: Goal-Setting as an Interaction Process," *American Sociological Review*, 23 (1958):23–31.

Van de Ven, Andrew, and Gordon Walker. "The Dynamics of Interorganizational Coordination," *Administrative Science Quarterly*, 29 (December 1984):598–621.

Wartick, Steven L., and Philip L. Cochran. "Evolution of the Corporate Social Performance Model," *Academy of Management Review*, 10 (1985):758–69.

Weidenbaum, M. L. *Business Government and the Public*. Englewood Cliffs, N.J.: Prentice-Hall, 1977.

Wood, D. J. *Strategic Use of Public Policy: Business and Government in the Progressive Era*. Boston: Pitman Publishing, 1985.

Writer's Guild of America, West, Inc. *v.* FCC, 423 F. Supp. 1064 (C.D. Cal. 1976).

INDEX

Academicians, 90
Accommodation, 115; strategies, 110
Accountability, 59, 64, 65, 117, 133
Action for Children's Television, 24
Activist posture for managers, 58
Adams, S. M., 73
Adjudication, 10, 11, 23, 31, 89
Administrative law judges (ALJs), 22
Administrative procedures, 10
Adversarial, 6, 67, 108; hypothesis, 27; model, 3, 6; proceedings, 16
Agency heads, 13
Agricultural programs, 20
ALJs (administrative law judges), 22
Allison, G. T., 75
Alternative strategies, 62
American law, 15
American management systems, 59, 64
Analytical approach, 2
Antecedents, 44
Anticipatory strategic posture, 62
Antitrust legislation, 4
Associations, private sector and government, 53
Aupperle, K., 43

Bargaining, 5
Baseless stereotypes, 122
Behavior of IORs, 61
Benchmarks, 71
BGR (business-government relations), 2, 4, 6, 11, 14, 24, 44, 53, 61, 76, 83, 103, 111, 123, 127, 131, 136; antipathies and aphorisms, 12; bifurcated, 59; collaboration, 5, 139; strategies, 47, 62, 68, 84, 89, 103, 130, 142
Big Business, 129
Bok, D., 4
Bottom-line mentality, 117
Boundaries of social needs, 60; permissible, 111
British common law, 15
Buchholz, R. A., 4
Bureaucracy bashing, 63, 74, 116, 117, 132
Business, 14, 64. See also Big Business; BGR; Corporations
Business-government relations. See BGR
Business media, 4
Businessmen, 3
Business Week, 40

Cause-effect of interdependence, 61
Centralized government, 57
CEOs, 13
Checks and balances system, 22
Chemical leaks, 117
Child labor legislation, 4
Civil servants, 117
Co-consultants, 12, 13, 77, 116, 118
Co-optation, 5, 22
Co-participation/co-determination, 63

About the Authors

JOHN M. STEVENS is an Associate Professor in the Department of Public Administration at the Pennsylvania State University and is also the Graduate Program Officer in the Policy Analysis Program. He is the coauthor of *Information Systems and Public Management* (Praeger, 1985) and the author of articles appearing in the *Academy of Management Journal*, *Public Administration Review*, *Journal of Management*, *Policy Studies Review*, *Research in Higher Education*, *Public Productivity Review*, and *Journal of Police Science and Administration*, among others.

STEVEN L. WARTICK is Assistant Professor of Business Administration at the Pennsylvania State University. He is the author or coauthor of over thirty articles that have been published in such journals as the *Academy of Management Review*, *California Management Review*, *Business Horizons*, and the *Social Science Journal*.

JOHN W. BAGBY is an Associate Professor of Business Law at the Pennsylvania State University. His research has been published in over fifteen scholarly journals, including *Harvard Business Review*, *Georgia Law Review*, *Securities Regulation Law Journal*, *Corporate Information and Privacy Law Reporter*, *American Business Law Journal*, *Accounting Horizons*, *C.P.A. Journal*, *Transportation Journal*, and *New England Law Review*, among others.

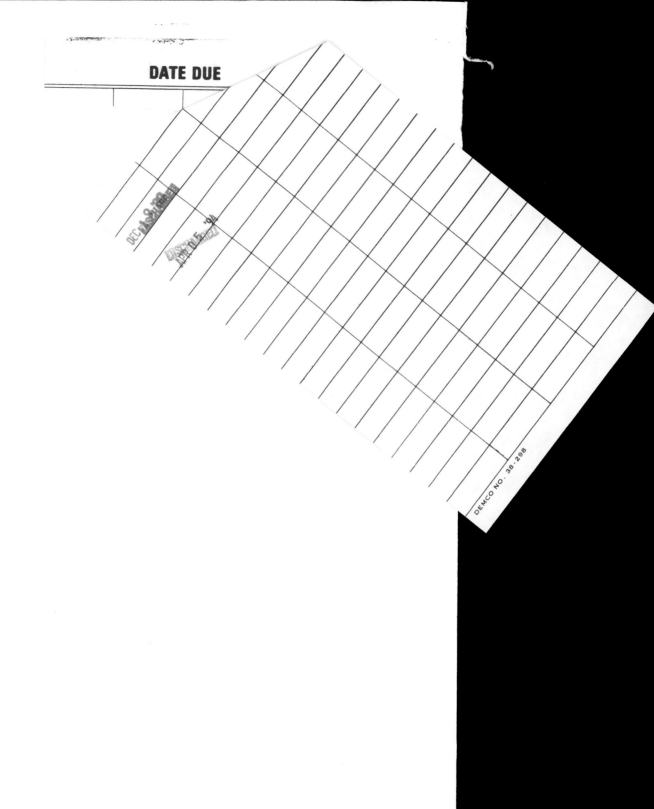